Lecture Notes in Computer Science　13181

More information about this series at https://link.springer.com/bookseries/558

Xiaoming Li · Sunita Chandrasekaran (Eds.)

Languages and Compilers for Parallel Computing

34th International Workshop, LCPC 2021
Newark, DE, USA, October 13–14, 2021
Revised Selected Papers

Springer

Editors
Xiaoming Li 🆔
Department of Electrical and Computer
Engineering
University of Delaware
Newark, DE, USA

Sunita Chandrasekaran 🆔
Department of Computer Science
University of Delaware
Newark, DE, USA

ISSN 0302-9743   ISSN 1611-3349 (electronic)
Lecture Notes in Computer Science
ISBN 978-3-030-99371-9   ISBN 978-3-030-99372-6 (eBook)
https://doi.org/10.1007/978-3-030-99372-6

This Springer imprint is published by the registered company Springer Nature Switzerland AG
The registered company address is: Gewerbestrasse 11, 6330 Cham, Switzerland

Preface

It's our pleasure to report the papers accepted for the 34th International Workshop on Languages and Compilers for Parallel Computing (LCPC 2021) held during October 13–14, 2021. The workshop was planned to be hosted physically in Newark, Delaware, USA, but was changed to a virtual event due to the COVID-19 situation at the time of the workshop.

Since 1986, LCPC has become a valuable venue for researchers to report research in the general areas of parallel computing, high-performance computer architecture, and compilers. LCPC 2021 continued this tradition and offered a highly interactive forum for the dissemination of innovative research contributions as well as in-depth discussions of novel and emerging ideas. As in past years, LCPC 2021 brought together researchers from academia, national labs, and industry with the aim of creating and strengthening research collaborations. In particular, this year's workshop extended the area of interest to new high-performance computing paradigms such as such as deep learning and autonomous vehicles.

We were fortunate to have a diverse set of 20 expert Program Committee (PC) members, spanning junior and senior researchers, women and under-represented groups, and researchers from a cross section of the community, including academia, industry, and national labs.

This year we received 12 submissions from authors in five countries. Each submission received at least four reviews and most had five reviews. The PC also sought additional external reviews for contentious papers. The review process was guided by novelty; reviewers were given explicit instructions to look for novel, intriguing ideas in the submissions. The inclusion of papers that propose new ideas – a new problem, a new research topic, radical insight into an existing topic, surprising results, etc. – was one of the key goals in devising the workshop program. Another important consideration was whether the paper could provoke interesting discussions during the workshop. Regardless of acceptance or rejection, authors were provided with detailed feedback. The PC held extensive online discussions during the week of August 23 to discuss the papers. Using an online system, this reviewing process was double-blind with PC members who had a conflict of interest being separated from discussion. From the 12 submissions, the PC selected 10 full papers to be included in the workshop proceedings. As in past LCPC workshops, a two-phase revision process was followed for the accepted papers. First, the authors were asked to incorporate the reviewers' feedback and prepare a pre-proceedings version of the paper, which was made available at the workshop. Next, the authors were asked to incorporate the feedback received during the workshop and prepare a final camera-ready version, which is included in this proceedings.

We were fortunate to have two keynote speeches, two invited talks, and a panel discussion in this year's workshop.

The first keynote talk was given by Shaoshan Liu, Founder and CEO of PerceptIn Inc., with the title "Building Computing Systems for Autonomous Machines: How Can Compiler Help?". Liu shared their experiences of building computing systems for autonomous machines, including on-machine computing systems, cloud computing systems, and cooperative autonomous machine computing systems (e.g., multi robots). Based on these case studies, he summarized their key findings and explored how compilers can help guarantee the real-time performance, reliability, safety, and security of autonomous machines.

The second keynote talk, "Systems 2030: The Extended Reality Case" presented by Sarita Adve from the University of Illinois at Urbana-Champaign, reviewed the end of Dennard scaling and Moore's law. Adve introduced their recently released ILLIXR — Illinois Extended Reality testbed— the first open source XR system and testbed for XR systems research. Building ILLIXR makes it evident that the systems of 2030 require researchers to learn how to do application-driven, end-to-end quality of experience-driven, and hardware-software-application co-designed systems research.

Michelle Mills Strout from the University of Arizona and HPE gave the first invited talk on "Separating Parallel Performance Concerns Using Chapel". In the talk, Mills suggested that to empower programmers to make decisions about implementation details at a higher level, we need a programming system that cleanly separates WHAT the code is trying to do, from HOW it should accomplish it in terms of data and computation organization. This talk showed how the Chapel parallel programming language achieves this clean separation by enabling multiresolution programming.

The second invited talk was presented by Zhijia Zhao, from UC Riverside, with the title "Program Parallelization - A Finite-State Machine-Centric Approach". A Finite-State Machine (FSM) is a basic computation model widely used for many applications. However, due to the inherent dependences among state transitions, it is very challenging to parallelize FSM-based computations. Zhao introduced several basic techniques for parallelizing FSM-based computations, including both enumerative parallelization and speculative parallelization, and demonstrated the conversion of bitstream computations to FSM computations with the help of a series of program analyses and dependence modeling techniques.

A special panel was held on October 14 to stimulate the discussion among junior researchers and new graduates on "Life after leaving the Advisor's Nest". The panel was moderated by Marton Kong from the University of Oklahoma, with the participation of Riyadh Baghdadi (NYU Abu Dhabi), Doru Popovici (Lawrence Berkeley National Laboratory), Naser Sedaghati (Cruise) and Richard Veras (University of Oklahoma). The panelists answered questions about how to jump start your research and career after leaving grad school and shared their early job experiences, responsibilities, and strategies to expand their network of collaborators.

We would like to thank the many people whose valuable time and effort made LCPC 2021 a success. We first want to thank all authors who contributed papers to the workshop. Furthermore, the success of LCPC is unimaginable without the passionate commitment of the Steering Committee, as well as the great effort of the Program Committee members and external reviewers. We also want to express our gratitude to the networking session chair, Martin Kong (University of Oklahoma), and the publication chair, Sanhu Li (University of Delaware), who made significant contributions to the quality organization of the workshop.

October 2021   Xiaoming Li
                                                                 Sunita Chandrasekaran

Organization

Workshop Chairs

Xiaoming Li   University of Delaware, USA
Sunita Chandrasekaran   University of Delaware, USA

Program Committee

Jose Nelson Amaral   University of Alberta, Canada
Prasanth Chatarasi   IBM, USA
William Godoy   Oak Ridge National Laboratory, USA
Lei Huang   Prairie View A&M University, USA
Paul Kelly   Imperial College London, UK
Keiji Kimura   Waseda University, Japan
Martin Kong   University of Oklahoma, USA
Seyong Lee   Oak Ridge National Laboratory, USA
Hatem Ltaief   King Abdullah University of Science and
                                 Technology, Saudi Arabia
Joseph Manzano   Pacific Northwest National Laboratory, USA
Georgios Markomanolis   CSC, Finland
Jose Manuel Monsalve Diaz   Argonne National Lab, USA
Stephen Olivier   Sandia National Laboratories, USA
Ivy Peng   Lawrence Livermore National Laboratory, USA
Sanjay Rajopadhye   Colorado State University, USA
Lawrence Rauchwerger   University of Illinois, USA
Maria Ruiz Varela   University of Delaware, USA
Angel de Vicente   Instituto de Astrofísica de Canarias, Spain
Weile Wei   Louisiana State University, USA
Zhijia Zhao   UC Riverside, USA

Networking Sessions Chair

Martin Kong   University of Oklahoma, USA

Publication Chair

Sanhu Li   University of Delaware, USA

Steering Committee

Rudolf Eigenmann	University of Delaware, USA
Alex Nicolau	UC Irvine, USA
David Padua	University of Illinois, USA
Lawrence Rauchwerger	Texas A&M University and University of Illinois, USA
Vivek Sarkar	Georgia Tech, USA

Contents

Compiler

Locality-Based Optimizations in the Chapel Compiler

Engin Kayraklioglu[✉], Elliot Ronaghan, Michael P. Ferguson,
and Bradford L. Chamberlain

Hewlett Packard Enterprise, Seattle, USA
{engin,elliot.ronaghan,michael.ferguson,blc}@hpe.com

Abstract. One of the main challenges of distributed memory programming is achieving efficient access to data. Low-level programming paradigms such as MPI and SHMEM require programmers to explicitly move data between compute nodes, which typically results in good execution performance at the expense of programmer productivity. High-level paradigms such as the Chapel programming language aim to reduce programming difficulty by supporting a global memory view. However, implicit communication afforded by the global memory view can make it easier for the programmers to overlook performance considerations. In this paper, we show that Chapel's high-level abstractions such as data-parallel loops and distributed arrays that enable easier programming can also enable powerful compiler analyses and optimizations, which can mitigate these overheads. We demonstrate two compiler optimizations added to the Chapel compiler in versions 1.23 and 1.24. These optimizations rely·on the use of data-parallel loops and distributed arrays to strength-reduce accesses to global memory and aggregate remote accesses. We test these optimizations with STREAM-Triad and index_gather benchmarks and show that they result in around 2x performance improvements on a Cray XC supercomputer. Furthermore, we analyze two real-world applications, chplUltra and Arkouda, that use manual remedies to address the overheads addressed by these optimizations. We observe that more than half of the places in the source code where these remedies are applied can benefit from optimizations without any programmer effort.

Keywords: Parallel programming · Compiler optimizations · Productivity

1 Introduction

Chapel is a parallel programming language that supports the partitioned global address space (PGAS) memory model. The PGAS model allows programmers to use a single namespace, which improves productivity by making all variables in the lexical scope accessible without explicit communication. Moreover, unlike other PGAS languages, Chapel's execution model is not SPMD by default. This implies that the variables in a given namespace refer to a single address in the

X. Li and S. Chandrasekaran (Eds.): LCPC 2021, LNCS 13181, pp. 3–17, 2022.
https://doi.org/10.1007/978-3-030-99372-6_1

global memory rather than different ones in each processing element. Chapel combines the PGAS memory model with other high-level concepts such as distributed arrays and data parallel distributed loops to create an expressive programming language.

Chapel's approach to distributed memory programming empowers several real-world applications. Chapel Multiphysics Software (CHAMPS) [18] is a CFD simulation library used for aircraft design and simulation and has close to 50 thousands lines of Chapel code. Arkouda [1] is a data-science-oriented Python library that is backed by a server implemented in Chapel for distributed memory programming. Arkouda has around 15 thousands lines of Chapel code. chplUltra [17] is an astrophysics software used for simulating the dynamics of ultralight dark matter and it consists of around 10 thousands lines of code.

On the other hand, developers using the PGAS model and high-level abstractions are prone to writing code with poor performance and scalability because of implicit communication. We show that common programming idioms supported by Chapel's high-level language concepts enable the compiler to perform automatic optimizations that would be impossible in low-level approaches such as message passing. Moreover, automatic optimizations based on high-level constructs tend to be portable as lower-level details are typically handled by the language runtime and communication middleware. This paper presents two such optimizations that significantly mitigate common performance overheads with no programmer effort. Specifically, our contributions are:

- design and implementation of an optimization where accesses to distributed arrays are made faster by avoiding locality checks in data-parallel loops
- design and implementation of an optimization that aggregates fine grained accesses in copy operations in data-parallel loops,
- experimental demonstration of performance improvements of these optimizations, and a discussion on their impact on real-world applications,
- discussion on how these optimizations and the Chapel compiler can be improved in general.

The rest of the paper is organized as follows. Section 2 gives a background on related Chapel concepts. Section 3 describes the two optimizations in detail. Section 4 shows some experimental and anecdotal results. Section 5 proposes future directions for the Chapel compiler and the optimizations presented here. Section 6 summarizes some related studies in the literature, and Sect. 7 concludes the paper.

2   Chapel Background

Our focus in this paper is on Chapel's high-level, data-parallel concepts. In this section, we give a short background on distributed arrays and `forall` loops in Chapel since both of these are key concepts for this work. For a more complete introduction to Chapel refer to [5].

2.1 Distributed Arrays

Chapel decouples an array's distribution from its data thanks to its *domain* concept. Domains are index sets that can describe how the indexed data should be mapped to the system memory. All Chapel arrays have domains. Listing 1 shows how a domain can be declared, and how it can be used to declare an integer array[1].

```
1  // a local, 1−based, m−by−n domain (index set)
2  var myDomain = {1..m, 1..n};
3
4  // an integer array declared over that domain
5  var myArray: [myDomain] int;
```

Listing 1. Declaring non-distributed domains and arrays in Chapel

To create a distributed array, one needs only to declare the domain as distributed by using a standard or a user-defined distribution [7]. Listing 2 shows how a block-distributed domain and array can be created in Chapel. Note that the array declaration is identical to that in Listing 1.

```
1  use BlockDist;
2  var myDomain = {1..m, 1..n} dmapped Block(....);
3  var myArray: [myDomain] real;
```

Listing 2. Declaring distributed domains and arrays in Chapel

Listing 3 shows some of the most common ways Chapel arrays can be accessed and manipulated. These include but not limited to; whole-array operations, iteration over their elements, and indexed accesses.

```
1  // using promoted or whole−array operations
2  myArray = 1.1;
3
4  // using sequential iteration over its elements
5  for elem in myArray do
6    elem = 2.2;
7
8  // using indexing (with sequential iteration over its domain)
9  for idx in myDomain do
10   myArray[idx] = 3.3;
```

Listing 3. Common ways of accessing a Chapel array serially

2.2 Forall Loops

Chapel has several kinds of loops in order to support different parallel programming patterns. One such loop is the `forall` loop. A `forall` loop can parallelize

---

[1] There are shorter syntactic alternatives for creating arrays without an explicit domain declaration, such as `var A: [1..n] int;`. Nonetheless, all Chapel arrays have domains.

6   E. Kayraklioglu et al.

and/or distribute the iteration across the system depending on the iterand that drives it. For example, a `forall` loop over a non-distributed domain or array would typically use all of the cores on the local compute node to implement the loop; whereas one over a distributed domain or array would use all of the cores on all of the compute nodes over which the array is distributed. Use of `forall`s in conjunction with distributed arrays and domains guarantees that loop iterations are distributed similarly to the data that it is iterating over. This observation is key in implementing locality-based optimizations in the compiler.

Listing 4 shows the `forall` version of the two loops previously shown in Listing 3.

```
1  // using parallel/distributed iteration over its elements
2  forall elem in myArray do
3    elem = 2.2;
4
5  // using indexing (with parallel/distributed iteration over its domain)
6  forall idx in myDomain do
7    myArray[idx] = 3.3;
```

Listing 4. `forall` Loops Over Domains and Arrays

Note that the only syntactical difference from the loops shown in Listing 3 is the use of keyword `forall` instead of `for`.

3 Compiler Analysis and Optimizations

In this section, we first describe the automatic local access optimization that analyzes `forall` loops to determine local array accesses, and avoids dynamic locality checks for those accesses. This optimization is implemented in Chapel version 1.23 and it is on-by-default. Second, we summarize the automatic aggregation optimization that aggregates communication in the last statements in `forall` loop bodies. This optimization is added to the Chapel compiler in version 1.24, and can be enabled with the `--auto-aggregation` flag.

3.1 Automatic Local Access

Accesses to Chapel arrays are implemented with a method named `this` on the array type that is automatically called by the compiler. A simplified implementation of `this` for a distributed array type is shown in Listing 5.

```
1  proc this(idx) {
2    if isLocalIndex(idx) then
3      return localAccess(idx);
4    else
5      return nonLocalAccess(idx);
6  }
```

Listing 5. A simplified implementation of distributed array access

Note that, in line 2, the implementation checks whether idx is local, because if it is, the array element can be accessed in a faster manner. However, this check itself has some small but noticeable overhead. The overhead is exacerbated if arrays are accessed in a tight inner loop—as is typically the case for conditionals inside such loops. Consider a STREAM-Triad [23] implementation in Chapel that uses indexed access into distributed arrays, as shown in Listing 6.

```
1  use BlockDist;
2  var Dom = {1..n} dmapped Block(....);
3  var A, B, C: [Dom] int;
4
5  forall i in Dom do
6    A[i] = B[i] + alpha * C[i];
```

Listing 6. STREAM-Triad kernel with indexed access

In this snippet, the three distributed arrays are accessed by index in the forall loop body, and they would normally incur the locality checks as discussed above. However, these checks are provably unnecessary because:

- All three distributed arrays are accessed at the ith index, which is the loop index
- All arrays are distributed the same way as the loop's domain is distributed
- The forall loop will distribute the work in the same way the loop's domain (Dom) is distributed

The automatic local access optimization implemented in the Chapel compiler uses similar reasoning to improve the performance of local accesses to distributed arrays.

Finding Candidate Expressions for Optimization. Early in compilation, array accesses are simply call expressions that are indistinguishable from procedure calls[2]. On the other hand, by the time call expressions are resolved, and array accesses are differentiated, Chapel's AST is transformed significantly enough to make some of this analysis difficult. Therefore, during earlier compilation passes, we analyze and transform the AST, replacing all call expressions that are candidate for optimizations with a special compiler primitive. Listing 7 sketches a simplified version of how this initial analysis and call replacement works.

First, we iterate over all forall loops in the program. For each, we try to find the loop domain. A forall can iterate over a domain, which directly becomes the domain of the loop; or it can iterate over a domain query on an array (e.g. myArray.domain), in which case we try to find the array's declaration and deduce the domain from the declaration. If neither, we continue the analysis and try to optimize using dynamic checks (details are below).

---

[2] In Chapel, postfix parentheses and square brackets can be used interchangeably as long as the opening and closing delimiter is the same.

```
1 void findCandidates(loop) {
2   loopDom = findDomain(loop) // can return NULL
3   for call in loop.body.calls()
4     if (call.localityDominator == loop &&
5         call.arguments == loop.indices)
6       maybeArr = call.base
7       arrDom = findDomain(maybeArr) // can return NULL
8       static = ( loopDom != NULL &&
9                  arrDom != NULL &&
10                 loopDom == arrDom )
11      if static
12        loop.staticCandidates.insert(call)
13      else
14        loop.dynamicCandidates.insert(call)
15 }
```

Listing 7. Pseudocode for candidate discovery

Then, for every call inside the loop body which has the same argument(s) as the loop index(es), we assume that the called expression is an array symbol and try to find its domain. If we can find symbols representing the loop's domain and the array's domain and they are the same symbol, we say that this access is a *static candidate* for automatic local access optimization. If we couldn't find the domain for the loop and/or the array, this call is a *dynamic candidate* for automatic local access optimization. We add the call to the appropriate list of candidates.

Transforming AST For Static and Dynamic Checks. After finding candidates for the optimization, we transform the AST for the loop to add static and dynamic checks. Static checks are necessary because the initial analysis and transformation happens before type resolution. Therefore, we add static checks for both static and dynamic candidates, and they only check whether what we assumed to be an array symbol is actually an array symbol (as opposed to a procedure symbol) and the domain type supports this optimization. A requirement for supporting this optimization is that the domain distributes indices in the same way as it distributes a parallel iteration over itself. All the standard domain maps in Chapel support this optimization, but a user-defined domain map could be imagined where this is not the case. To provide a general solution, we expect domain maps to provide a function that returns a boolean at compile time that informs the compiler as to whether the domain map supports this optimization or not.

On the other hand, dynamic checks are added for cases where the relationship between the array and the loop domains cannot be established statically. This also supports cases where a forall only traverses a slice of an array's domain.

For a scenario where there is one static and one dynamic candidate, as in Listing 8, we create AST equivalent to that shown in Listing 9.

```
1 var dom1 = {1..n} dmapped Block (...);
2 var dom2 = {1..m} dmapped Block (...);
3 var arr1: [dom1] int, arr2: [dom2] int;
4
5 forall i in dom1 do
6   arr1[i] = arr2[i];
```

Listing 8. A case where arr1 and arr2 are static and dynamic candidates

```
1  // check all candidates statically:
2  if (staticCheck(arr1, loopDomain) &&
3      staticCheck(arr2, loopDomain)) then
4
5    // check dynamic candidates at execution time
6    if (dynamicCheck(arr2, loopDomain)) then
7      forall i in dom1 do
8        arr1.maybeLocal[i] = arr2.maybeLocal[i];
9    else
10     forall i in dom1 do
11       arr1.maybeLocal[i] = arr2[i];
12 else
13   forall i in dom1 do
14     arr1[i] = arr2[i];
```

Listing 9. Sketch of the generated AST for the snippet in Listing 8

The generated AST first does static checks on arrays that are optimization candidates. These checks are simple functions that return compile-time (in Chapel terminology, they are params) booleans. If all the candidates pass static checks, we dynamically check the dynamic candidates, as well. The first forall clone is where all static and dynamic candidates pass their checks, where the second is for the case for successful static, and failed dynamic checks. The final clone is identical to the user's loop, and does not have any optimizations.

Finalizing the Optimization. After the initial transformation is done, the generated AST is resolved more or less normally. Static checks are computed at compile time, and the conditional based on the static checks is folded. While resolving this AST, the only special case for this optimization is for resolving the maybeLocal calls. First, the compiler tries to resolve them as regular array accesses. If it can, it replaces them with a call to localAccess which avoids locality checks. If the compiler cannot resolve them as array accesses, they will be reverted to regular calls, and will be attempted to be resolved as such.

3.2 Automatic Aggregation

Another common overhead in PGAS languages occurs due to fine-grained communication. In some cases where the fine-grained access is predictable, caching and/or prefetching the remote data can help mitigate some of these overheads.

However, especially in cases where remote data is accessed randomly, such approaches are generally not very impactful. A solution for these scenarios is aggregating the communication and transferring data in bulk with fewer messages.

Listing 10 shows a simplified version of the *index_gather* kernel from the bale effort [2].

```
1 var cycArr = newCyclicArr(...);
2 var blockArr = newBlockArr(...);
3
4 fillRandom(blockArr);
5
6 var tmp: [blockArr.domain] int;
7
8 forall i in blockArr.domain do
9   tmp[i] = cycArr[blockArr[i]];
```
Listing 10. Simplified sketch of the index_gather kernel

The `forall` loop iterates over a block-distributed domain, while copying data from a cyclic-distributed array into a block-distributed one. In a straight-forward implementation, this element-wise, random-access copy operation causes fine-grained communication. However, this operation can be done in an aggregated fashion because:

- `tmp[i]` (and `blockArr[i]`) are local accesses because the `forall` is over the same domain as theirs. Furthermore, this will be recognized as such by the automatic local access optimization that was discussed in the previous section,
- Because `forall` is a parallel loop, individual copy operations that will execute at each iteration of the loop can be reordered without impacting the application behavior.

The automatic aggregation optimization implemented in the Chapel compiler will use reasoning along these lines in order to apply aggregation to optimize communication performance.

Locality Detection. Currently, automatic aggregation is supported only if the operation is a simple copy operation where one side is local and the other is not. To detect whether either side is local, we use the same approach and code as presented for automatic local access. In fact, there's a single analysis pass that collects enough locality information for both optimizations that are presented in this paper.

Avoiding Data Hazards. The aggregated copy operation requires order independence—that is, that the iterations of the optimized loop can run in any order including in parallel. In the context of the Chapel language, the `forall` loop implies that the loop body has this property. In addition, the aggregated copy operation only optimizes the last statements of loop bodies, because it implies that nothing in the loop body can depend on any writes that occur as a result of this statement. The Chapel compiler already had an optimization where such statements are executed in an unordered matter [8], and the automatic aggregation optimization uses the same analysis as the existing optimization.

Module Support. Aggregating communication requires allocating local buffers that can be used to store data temporarily before communicating and a mechanism to flush them as they fill up. Implementing this purely by compiler transformations is not very feasible. Instead, our optimization facilitates *Aggregator* objects that have been studied in Chapel before and have been heavily used in Arkouda, a data analytics software that is implemented in Chapel (server) and Python (client) [1].

Aggregators are module-level objects that represent per-task buffers that temporarily store data to be communicated along with their address. These objects are typically created as *task intent*. A loop using an Aggregator object typically uses a with clause to create one instance per task, as the following example shows:

```
1  forall i in myDomain with (var agg = new Aggregator(int)) {
2    ...
3    agg.copy(arr[i], data);  // equivalent to 'arr[i] = data'
4  }
5
```

Listing 11. Example of manual aggregator usage

Transformations. The forall loop in the index_gather kernel as shown in Listing 10 is transformed into something akin to Listing 12 early in compilation.

```
1  forall i in blockArr.domain with (var agg = new Aggregator(int)) do
2    if dummyAggregationMarker {
3      tmp[i] = cycArr[blockArr[i]];
4    }
5    else {
6      agg.copy(tmp[i], cycArr[blockArr[i]]);
7    }
```

Listing 12. Simplified transformation for automatic aggregation

Once hazard detection and other relevant passes, such as loop invariant code motion, are complete, we choose one of those branches and eliminate the other one. Therefore, there are no runtime checks of any sorts. Note that removing the else block also entails cleaning up any aggregator creation because they would be useless.

4   Results

We evaluate the performance of these optimizations by using the STREAM-Triad [23] and index_gather [2] benchmarks that motivate them. We compare the automatically-optimized execution time against their manually-optimized counterparts which were shown to perform comparably to reference MPI and SHMEM versions [9,10]. We also analyze the code for chplUltra [17] and Arkouda [1] to assess how the optimizations can improve them. We show that both of them cause straightforward implementations of benchmarks to perform similarly to manually-optimized versions. They also help avoid significant portion of the relevant manual optimizations in real-world applications.

We used a Cray XC30 supercomputer for the performance studies. Compute nodes are dual-socket and equipped with 36-core Broadwell CPUs clocked at 2.1 GHz. Nodes are connected with the Aries interconnect. Automatic local access comparisons were done against Chapel 1.23 pre-release, whereas automatic aggregation comparisons are against Chapel 1.24 pre-release[3], so that they capture the performance improvement introduced by the optimization on the release that they were implemented. We used the default configuration for all of these tests. The executables are compiled with --fast flag. In addition, the automatic aggregation tests are compiled with --auto-aggregation.

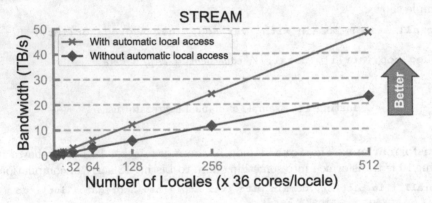

Fig. 1. STREAM-Triad bandwidth

Automatic Local Access. Figure 1 shows how this optimization improves STREAM-Triad performance. The kernel for this STREAM-Triad implementation is shown in Listing 13.

```
1 forall i in Dom do
2   A[i] = B[i] + alpha * C[i];
```

Listing 13. STREAM-Triad with indexed array access

---

[3] The most current Chapel release version is 1.24.1.

Without the automatic local access optimization, this kernel reaches only about half of system bandwidth (shown in dark blue with diamond markers), whereas other idioms for STREAM-Triad are able to reach the full system bandwidth. Other idioms are shown in Listings 14 and 15. The difference between the two types of idioms is that the distributed arrays are accessed by index in the first one, which causes overheads without the automatic local access optimization.

```
1  forall (a,b,c) in zip(A,B,C) do
2    a = b + alpha * c;
```

Listing 14. STREAM-Triad with zippered iteration over arrays

```
1  A = B + alpha * C;
```

Listing 15. STREAM-Triad with promoted expression

With this optimization, indexed STREAM-Triad performs about twice as fast, reaching the limits of the system. This performance is virtually identical to other idioms that do not use indexed access into distributed arrays.

In addition, we inspected the *chplUltra* [17] which relies on explicit use of localAccess for better performance. We have observed that, thanks to the automatic local access optimization, we can reduce the number of explicit calls to localAccess from 80 to 21, without sacrificing performance. The remaining explicit localAccess calls are either not within forall loops, or the index that they access is a function of the loop index.

Automatic Aggregation. Figure 2 shows that without any optimization, the index-gather benchmark, shown in Listing 10 does not scale (light blue, dashed line, square markers). The unordered forall optimization [8], firing automatically with no user effort, improves performance by enabling out-of-order communication (medium blue). Finally, manual aggregation (dark blue) and automatic aggregation (solid green) perform very similarly and much better than the other versions, where the latter does not require any user effort at all.

To explore the impact of this optimization in user code, we analyzed Arkouda, the application for which user-level aggregators were implemented initially. Thanks to the automatic aggregation optimization, we were able to reduce the number of explicit aggregators from 61 to 22. The most common causes for the remaining 22 are identical to those limitations of the automatic local access optimization: (1) operation is not inside a forall or (2) the array access index is complicated. These two causes require 12 of the remaining 22 cases to use explicit aggregation. The remaining 10 require more investigation.

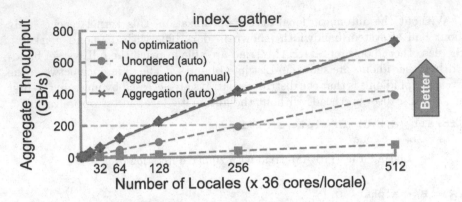

Fig. 2. Bale index_gather (Color figure online)

5   Future Work

We want to investigate extending the automatic local access optimization to handle array accesses where the index is an affine expression based on the loop index. Such accesses are common in linear algebra codes, and currently are not covered by this optimization. Furthermore, many loops in applications use for and coforall[4] loops and it would benefit these cases to extend the optimization beyond forall loops. These other loops do not have any guarantees about data locality, however, there are common idioms where they are used in a way that can benefit from this optimization.

As of Chapel 1.24, automatic aggregation is off-by-default and can be enabled by the --auto-aggregation flag. There are two main concerns for enabling it by default. First, the aggregator objects are not designed for handling all-local aggregation. This is because the initial use case for them was for the programmer to explicitly use them and with the assumption that they would use them only if they know for sure that there is communication. However, the compiler can automatically use aggregation in cases where both sides of a copy is actually local, even though some of the static analysis tries to prevent that. We observed that there can be around 2x slowdown in such cases. However, we believe that we can adjust the aggregator implementation to reduce the overhead in such cases. Second, aggregators use per-locale buffers on each Chapel task (typically a core). This poses issues when aggregators are used in systems with high locale and core counts. We would like to consider reducing the memory overhead of aggregators, potentially using multi-hop aggregation where some local aggregation takes place before communicating the data, thereby reducing its memory footprint.

The automatic aggregation optimization covers assignments that are the last statements in the loop bodies. This coverage can be expanded in two ways. First, we can support arbitrary operations to be aggregated. This would mean creating function pointers representing the operation and using that function to unpack

---

[4] A loop where each iteration is mapped to a parallel Chapel task.

the aggregated data instead of just copying them in local memory. Second, this optimization can cover all statements inside the loop body. This requires alias and dataflow analysis inside the loop body to avoid data dependences.

6 Related Work

A relatively early study on how high-level language constructs can enable compiler optimizations is done by Choi and Snyder [12]. The authors show that array operations like shifts can be efficiently optimized by the compiler, if the language enables expressing such operations using high-level constructs, such as operators. This work is based on ZPL [6], an array programming language. However, unlike Chapel, ZPL was not a general-purpose language. As such it did not support operations like array indexing.

Hayashi et al. [14] implemented several LLVM optimizations for Chapel programs to reduce costs associated with distributed memory programming. The authors focus on GET/PUT operations injected by the Chapel compiler and try to find ways in which they can be coalesced or eliminated. These optimizations achieve significant performance improvements. Currently, some of the optimizations presented in this work can be used with an experimental flag --llvm-wide-opt. These optimizations focus on communication calls that happen inside a lexical scope and do not consider calls that can be invoked repeatedly inside a loop.

Other distributed memory optimizations have been studied in the contexts of other PGAS languages with compilers. Chen et al. [11] describes strength-reduction, communication and computation overlap and message coalescing techniques in the Berkeley UPC compiler. We believe that the set of optimizations presented in this work are thematically similar to those that were studied by Hayashi et al.

Other studies pertaining Chapel's performance include but not limited to; runtime optimizations, such as caching [13], prefetching [16], inspector/executor optimizations [20], profile-based optimizations [15]; module optimizations, such as iteration reorganization [3], complex bulk transfer [21]; GPU-related explorations [4], and finally general performance studies in comparison with other programming models [22].

Single-node loop optimizations for improving data access performance are common. A significant portion of the literature focuses on loop and data layout transformations based on the polyhedral model for related optimizations such as auto-vectorization [24] and improved cache utilization [19]. We believe, similar techniques can be used in the Chapel compiler. However, they typically focus on affine array accesses in loops which are not in scope for this paper.

7 Conclusion

In this paper, we show that well-designed high-level language abstractions not only make programming easier, but can also express key information about the application that can enable powerful compiler optimizations. To demonstrate this point, we present two optimizations added to the Chapel compiler in recent releases that have been used in production-level applications. The first optimization, automatic local access, reduces the costs of accessing local parts of a distributed array. The second optimization, automatic aggregation, gathers communication operations locally before communicating them in bulk. Both of these optimizations are enabled by high-level concepts like `forall` loops and distributed arrays. They both can increase performance without adding any programming burden in benchmarks and real-world applications alike.

Acknowledgement. We would like to thank Michelle Strout for reviewing an early draft and sharing very valuable insights that contributed to this paper's quality.

References

1. Arkouda: NumPy-like arrays at massive scale backed by Chapel. https://github. com/Bears-R-Us/arkouda. Accessed 26 Jul 2021
2. Bale. https://github.com/jdevinney/bale. Accessed 26 Jul 2021
3. Bertolacci, I.J., et al.: Parameterized diamond tiling for stencil computations with chapel parallel iterators. In: Proceedings of the 29th ACM on International Conference on Supercomputing, ICS 2015, pp. 197–206. ACM (2015). ISBN 978-1-4503-3559-1. https://doi.org/10.1145/2751205.2751226
4. Carneiro, T., et al.: Towards Chapel-based Exascale Tree Search Algorithms: dealing with multiple GPU accelerators. In: HPCS 2020, p. 9 (2021)
5. Chamberlain, B.L.: Chapel, chap. 6. In: Balaji, P. (ed.) Programming Models for Parallel Computing, pp. 129–159. MIT Press (2015)
6. Chamberlain, B.L.: The design and implementation of a region based parallel programming language. University of Washington (2001)
7. Chamberlain, B.L., et al.: User-defined distributions and layouts in Chapel: philosophy and framework. In: Proceedings of the 2nd USENIX Conference on Hot Topics in Parallelism, HotPar 2010, p. 12. USENIX Association (2010)
8. Chapel 1.20 Release Notes: Benchmarks and Performance Optimizations. https:// chapellang.org/releaseNotes/1.20/06-perf-opt.pdf. Accessed 26 Jul 2021
9. Chapel 1.23 Release Notes: Ongoing Efforts. https://chapel-lang.org/releaseNotes/ 1.23/05-ongoing.pdf. Accessed 26 Jul 2021
10. Chapel: Performance Highlights: STREAM Triad. https://chapel-lang.org/perf-stream.html. Accessed 26 Jul 2021
11. Chen, W.-Y., Iancu, C., Yelick, K.: Communication optimizations for fine-grained UPC applications. In: 14th International Conference on Parallel Architectures and Compilation Techniques, PACT 2005, pp. 267–278. IEEE (2005)
12. Choi, S.-E., Snyder, L.: Quantifying the effects of communication optimizations. In: Proceedings of the 1997 International Conference on Parallel Processing (Cat. No. 97TB100162), August 1997, pp. 218–222 (1997). https://doi.org/10.1109/ICPP. 1997.622647
13. Ferguson, M.P., Buettner, D.: Caching puts and gets in a PGAS language runtime. In: 2015 9th International Conference on Partitioned Global Address Space Programming Models, September 2015, pp. 13–24 (2015). https://doi.org/10.1109/ PGAS.2015.10

14. Hayashi, A., et al.: LLVM-based communication optimizations for PGAS programs. In: LLVM 2015, pp. 1–11. ACM Press (2015). ISBN 978-1-4503-4005-2. https://doi.org/10.1145/2833157.2833164

15. Kayraklioglu, E., Favry, E., El-Ghazawi, T.: A machine-learning-based framework for productive locality exploitation. IEEE Trans. Parallel Distrib. Syst. **32**(6), 1409–1424 (2021). https://doi.org/10.1109/TPDS.2021.3051348

16. Kayraklioglu, E., Ferguson, M.P., El-Ghazawi, T.: LAPPS: locality-aware productive prefetching support for PGAS. ACM Trans. Archit. Code Optim. **15**(3), 28:1-28:26 (2018). https://doi.org/10.1145/3233299

17. Padmanabhan, N., et al.: Simulating ultralight dark matter in Chapel. In: 2020 IEEE International Parallel and Distributed Processing Symposium Workshops (IPDPSW), May 2020, pp. 678–678 (2020). https://doi.org/10.1109/IPDPSW50202.2020.00120

18. Parenteau, M., et al.: Development of parallel CFD applications with the Chapel programming language. In: AIAA Scitech 2021 Forum. American Institute of Aeronautics and Astronautics (2021). https://doi.org/10.2514/6.2021-0749

19. Patwardhan, A.A., Upadrasta, R.: PolyhedralModel guided automatic GPU cache exploitation framework. In: 2019 International Conference on High Performance Computing Simulation (HPCS), pp. 496–503 (2019). https://doi.org/10.1109/HPCS48598.2019.9188095

20. Rolinger, T.B., Krieger, C.D., Sussman, A.: Runtime optimizations for irregular applications in Chapel. https://chapel-lang.org/CHIUW/2021/Rolinger.pdf. Accessed 26 Jul 2021

21. Sanz, A., et al.: Global data re-allocation via communication aggregation in Chapel. In: 2012 IEEE 24th International Symposium on Computer Architecture and High Performance Computing (SBAC-PAD), October 2012, pp. 235–242 (2012). https://doi.org/10.1109/SBAC-PAD.2012.18

22. Slaughter, E., et al.: Task bench: a parameterized benchmark for evaluating parallel runtime performance. In: Proceedings of the International Conference for High Performance Computing, Networking, Storage and Analysis. IEEE Press (2020). ISBN 9781728199986

23. STREAM Benchmark Reference Information. http://www.cs.virginia.edu/stream/ref.html. Accessed 26 Jul 2021

24. Trifunovic, K., et al.: Polyhedral-model guided loop-nest auto-vectorization. In: 2009 18th International Conference on Parallel Architectures and Compilation Techniques, pp. 327–337 (2009). https://doi.org/10.1109/PACT.2009.18

iCetus: A Semi-automatic Parallel Programming Assistant

Parinaz Barakhshan[✉] [iD] and Rudolf Eigenmann[iD]

University of Delaware, Newark, DE 19716, USA
{parinazb,eigenman}@udel.edu

Abstract. The iCetus tool is a new interactive parallelizer, providing users with a range of capabilities for the source-to-source transformation of C programs using OpenMP directives in shared memory machines. While the tool can parallelize code fully automatically for non-experts, power users can steer the parallelization process in a menu-driven way. iCetus which is still in its early stages of development is implemented as a web application for easy access, eliminating the need for user installation and updates. The tool supports the user through all phases of the program transformation process, including program analyses, parallelization, and optimization. The first phase includes both static and dynamic analyses, pointing out loops that represent performance bottlenecks and should be improved. The parallelization phase offers diverse options to cater to different levels of user skills. By displaying compiler analyses results in an interactive manner, iCetus supports the user in pinpointing parallelization impediments and resolving them. During the optimization phase, the programmer can apply successive improvements by editing the program, evaluating the performance, and comparing it to that obtained by previous program versions. iCetus also serves as a learning tool to help users understand important program patterns and their parallelization. In this way, it also helps train the user in writing code that likely yields better performance.

Keywords: Interactive source-to-source compiler · OpenMP parallel programming model · Shared memory architecture · Code optimization · Code parallelization

1 Introduction

With the advent of multi-core architectures, the need to fully utilize the capabilities of a computer system has become a topic of great concern among application developers. Given the difficulties of mastering the skills of manually writing high-quality parallel code, many attempts have been made in the past to automate the process of converting sequential to parallel programs. Despite more than four decades of research in automatic program parallelization and although nearly all of today's computer architectures are parallel, current software engineers still make little use of automatic parallelization tools.

© Springer Nature Switzerland AG 2022
X. Li and S. Chandrasekaran (Eds.): LCPC 2021, LNCS 13181, pp. 18–32, 2022.
https://doi.org/10.1007/978-3-030-99372-6_2

The state-of-the-art parallelizer is a batch-oriented optimizing compiler that offers its users little guidance for and control over its operation, except for a sizeable number of command-line options.

Typically, parallelizing compilers are able to extract parallelism in about one in two science/engineering applications. While this is a success from a science viewpoint, it is unsatisfactory to the end user. It is especially aggravating for the engineer of novel applications, which may not exhibit the regular data structures that parallelization technology learned to optimize well.

What's more, even where the tools succeed in detecting parallelism, mapping this parallelism to a given architecture may introduce overheads that offset the gain of automatic optimization. The result is that users see large performance variations across programs and architectures, ranging from nearly ideal speedup to significant slowdown compared to the original program.

From a compiler point of view this problem has two major reasons:

1. Parallelization techniques are highly complex and user code may obscure parallelism. Furthermore, we demand that compilers perform their optimizations correctly on *all* programs. The latter is different from how we think about parallel programming models. For example, OpenMP permits its users to parallelize a loop even if there is a race condition. It is the user's responsibility if the execution is incorrect. The strict demand for correctness makes parallelizers conservative, bypassing many opportunities for optimization. The demand also prevents transformations that are considered *unsafe*. These are transformations that may produce a different, but user-acceptable result than the original code.

2. Every program transformation introduces overhead. Estimating this overhead is highly complex and depends on characteristics of both the program and the target architecture. Performance models usually include parameters that are only known once the program executes, making it often infeasible for the compiler to decide whether or not an applicable technique is beneficial. The dilemma is that not applying the technique forgoes the optimization opportunity; applying it, may introduce overhead that offsets the gain or, worse, degrades performance.

An additional issue motivating the present work is that teaching the skills of program parallelization lacks educational tools that illustrate concepts, program analyses & transformations, and report performance results in an intuitive way.

How can we work around these problems?

- *Parallel Programming Models:* Writing a program using parallel programming models, without automatic parallelization, gives full control to the software engineer. This route may be desirable for experienced programmers but is often prohibitive for domain scientists and engineers focusing on their physics, chemistry, or biology, rather than program parallelization.
- *Auto-tuning:* Platforms have been proposed that try many optimization variants for a given program and data sets, picking the best. Doing so can

be extremely time-consuming, due to the combinatorial complexity of trying the many program optimization variants. What's more, tailoring such a platform to a user's specific compilation and execution environment can take a prohibitive number of engineering parameters. As a result, no available parallelizer today offers a general auto-tuning platform.

- *Hardware Support:* Hardware solutions can significantly reduce parallelization overhead and enable certain unsafe optimizations. For example, architectures have explored support for instruction-level launch of parallel loops (substantially reducing the loop fork-join cost - a major parallelization overhead), loop-level synchronization (enabling low-overhead parallel execution of loops with dependences), and speculative parallelization (overcoming some of compilers' conservative assumptions). While these techniques are known, engineering trade offs so far have prevented them from becoming part of modern computer architectures.

- *Interactive Parallelization:* The approach pursued in this paper is to equip a parallelizing compiler with the ability to interact with the users, involving the user into the decisions that compilers struggle with. The idea is to consider user feedback in program parallelization. The objectives include (1) providing the user with information about how the compiler analyzes, transforms, and parallelizes the program, and (2) creating an interface for controlling program parallelization, based on this feedback. Doing so combines user knowledge and compiler capabilities. This information will also help the programmer to write code that is more amenable to automatic parallelization as well as help the student understand the involved techniques and their interactions.

While there are several early projects exploring interactive parallel optimization, which will be discussed in Sect. 5, to the best of our knowledge, no interactive tool exists that harnesses the power of today's most successful automatic parallelizers. This project builds on the Cetus parallelizer, which has shown to be the most effective, making its capabilities available for interactive use. The paper presents an initial design of iCetus and then discusses and evaluates features requested by an early user community.

The rest of the paper is organized as follows. Section 2 explains automatic parallelization, the opportunity of interactive parallelization, the features of iCetus, and the limitations of the current version of iCetus. Section 3 describes the iCetus implementation. Section 4 evaluates existing as well as proposed iCetus features. Section 5 discusses related work and Sect. 6 presents conclusions.

2   Rationale for the iCetus Interactive Parallelizer and Tool Features

This section provides a brief overview of the capabilities of automatic parallelization (Sect. 2.1) and then describes how the provision of these capabilities in an interactive manner can address the issues described in the introduction (Sect. 2.2). Section 2.3 presents the features of iCetus through an example.

2.1   Automatic Parallelization in Cetus

The iCetus tool is based on the Cetus parallelizing compiler infrastructure [2]. Cetus performs source-to-source translation, converting C source code into equivalent C code, annotated with OpenMP parallel directives.

To do so, Cetus applies a number of compilation passes that we classify into program analysis, parallel loop transformations, and performance optimization techniques. This classification is not strict, serving just the presentation of this paper. Program analysis passes include range analysis, alias analysis, points-to analysis, private variable analysis, reduction variable analysis, induction variable analysis, and data dependence analysis. Parallel loop transformations use the analysis information to determine which loops can safely be executed in parallel, annotate these loops as such (using Cetus-internal pragmas), and transform induction and reduction expressions into their parallel forms, as needed. Performance optimizations deal with the efficient mapping of the identified parallel loops to the target architecture. The involved techniques include loop interchange, tiling, and profitability analysis.

The above description is simplified for the presentation of this paper. Additional passes bring the code into a normalized form for easier analysis and transformation. Also, some passes may be split, such as the actual parallel reduction expressions being inserted only after profitability analysis has determined that the parallel execution of a given loop is beneficial.

Cetus generates a report documenting the passes it has applied and providing details on the operation and findings of the passes. Users can select the verbosity of this report via command line options. The highest verbosity level can generate an extensive optimization report.

2.2   The Opportunity of Interactive Parallelization

Recall from Sect. 1 the key problems of batch-oriented compilation, which are (1) conservative optimizations due to the requirement for absolute correctness, and (2) insufficient knowledge of the compiler for making informed decisions about which optimizations to beneficially apply to which program sections. Section 1 has also expressed the need for intuitive educational instruments. Here, we describe the opportunity for a tool that presents the capabilities of Sect. 2.1 interactively, addressing these challenges.

Correctness and Conservative Assumptions: Two key compiler capabilities in identifying parallelism are data dependence and private variable analysis. If a compiler cannot prove that data accesses are dependence free or variables are private, it conservatively assumes that they are not. Similar holds for other techniques, such as alias analysis, reduction parallelization, and induction variable recognition. What's more, certain loops may be correct in their parallel form, even if dependences provably exist. There may be a race condition that will lead to results that are different from the original sequential program, and different parallel executions may yield different results; but all these results may be algorithmically correct. An example is a search algorithm that finds a different one of multiple elements, all of which match the search criterion. Compilers must always create sequentially consistent results and thus cannot perform such transformations.

The opportunity for an interactive tool is to present the results of these analyses and then let the user decide what is acceptable. In this way, a data dependence that the compiler cannot disprove or a variable that the compiler cannot privatize can be tagged as such by the user. This is especially useful in the fairly common case of a loop where only a few hard-to-detect data dependence or private variable patterns remain that can be recognized by the user. Cetus' optimization report will be of help in this situation. By selectively showing the remaining dependences of a loop and allowing the user to drill down into the analysis details, an interactive tool can thus help parallelize key loop patterns that batch-oriented compilers are unable to.

Overheads and Profitability: A major reason that an automatically parallelized loop may execute more slowly than the original is that the loop is too small so that the cost of invoking and terminating the parallel activity dominates. Recall that not only is modelling the performance of a loop, transformed with potentially many techniques, highly complex, in most cases the model also includes parameters that depend on data read from a program input file and are thus unknown at compile time. The model could be evaluated at run-time, but such execution itself can introduce excessive overhead. We have observed that even using the seemingly low-overhead OpenMP conditional parallel loop construct (run in parallel if a certain condition holds) can yield low profitability. Transformations that add substantial code to the program, such as reduction parallelization and loop tiling, are especially prone to low profitability.

The opportunity for an interactive tool lies in informing the user about loops where profitability is borderline or needs run-time information. The tool can also disclose high-overhead transformations that have been applied, allowing the user to be the judge on profitability. While advanced users may have information that is not available to the compiler for such judgment, the task can still be arduous.

Another tool opportunity is to offer run-time measurements gained through program execution. The values of critical variables may be evaluated (e.g., the number of iterations of a loop), the execution time of a loop may be measured, or the performance of a serial and parallel code version may be compared. An advanced such scenario would be to "auto-tune" a code section or the entire program. That is, the interactive tool would execute many optimization variants and determine the best.

Educational Instrument: Teaching parallel programming techniques, their correctness, and their automation are highly complex. There are many involved concepts, program analyses that need to be understood, and transformations that need to be grasped. Tools that can illustrate these subjects, show the many aspects of program analyses and transformation with representative examples, and allow the student to play with what-if scenarios, can improve the learning experience tremendously.

2.3 iCetus Features

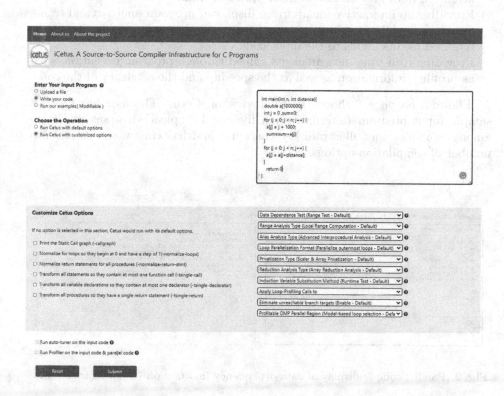

Fig. 1. Front view of iCetus, available at http://icetus.ece.udel.edu/cetusWeb/. The availability as a web tool obviates the need for download, install and version updates.

Building on the Cetus source-to-source restructurer, the tool displays the parallelized version of a given program in the form of OpenMP-annotated source code. The tool allows the user to observe the applied transformations and can serve as a starting point for further, manual optimizations.

iCetus is developed with the purpose of extending the capabilities of the Cetus compiler. Our intention is not to present just a user-friendly interface to the Cetus compiler, but to convert an automatic compiler to an interactive one. The followings are key features of the current iCetus prototype:

- iCetus is developed as a web application, in order to make it easier for the user to interact with it. Such an implementation introduces lots of benefits like cross-platform availability, portability, no need for installation, automatic updates, and being light on client-side computer resources since all processing would be done on server-side resources.
- Making the parallelization process easily customizable in a menu-driven and interactive way.

- Making the optimization process less error-prone by guiding the programmer's attention to the regions that hinder parallelization.
- Providing an interactive menu-driven display of program analyses and transformations while enabling the user to act on that information and make required modifications to the input code.
- Providing Run-time measurements gained through program execution, such as profiling information as well as the speedup and the efficiency of the code.

Figure 1, on page 6 shows the front view of iCetus. The user has typed a sample input program (alternatively a file can be uploaded or selected from among examples that illustrate key concepts) and has chosen to customize a number of compilation options.

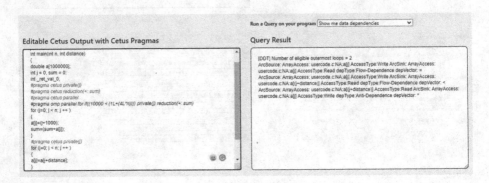

Fig. 2. Parallel code & display of data dependency information (Color figure online)

Figure 2 illustrates the menu-driven display of program analysis results. In the given program that is displayed on the left side, the second loop is not parallelized and is marked yellow. Color coding is applied to the output for showing the loop that is not parallelized to the user. That's why the second "for" loop is highlighted yellow. Given that information, the user has chosen to look at the existing data dependences from the drop-down menu. This menu is designed to let the user easily query the result of different analyses performed by the compiler on the given program. This feature not only helps the user identify the impediments of parallelization but also displays the performance gain from applying parallelization. Based on the query passed by the user, the report on the right side of the screen updates. In this case, a *flow-dependency* between a[j] and a[j+distance] with dependence Vector of "<" in the second loop is displayed. In this example, the compiler does not know about the value of variables "n" and "distance", and it reports on the dependency that might exist in between a[j] and a[j+distance], in which the "j" variable increases from "0" to "n" in steps of 1.

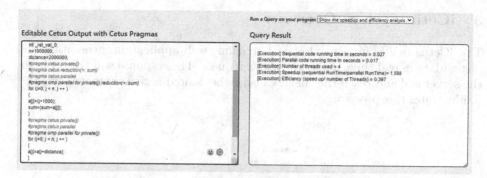

Fig. 3. Determining performance and efficiency

By providing a greater value to variable *"distance" comparing to variable* "n" the user manages to resolve the loop-carried flow dependency. Figure 3 shows the speedup and efficiency gained by the transformations after parallelizing both loops. The resources for this program execution are part of the web server, executing in a sandbox environment for security reasons.

The tool allows the user to edit and re-compile the resulting code. In this case, the data dependence is removed, turning the second loop into a parallel region as well. Recomputing the speedup shows the effect of this program improvement immediately.

2.4 Limitations of the Current Version of iCetus

Recall that iCetus is still in the early stages of its development. Some of the current limitations are given below; they will be resolved in future versions.

- The current version only accepts a source code from the user. It does not accept any data input file.
- The given program should be self-contained, meaning it must include all header files that contain developer definitions. The header files that come with the compiler are recognized by the tool, however.
- Computational resources for program executions to obtain profile runs and other dynamic measurements are limited to a small machine.
- The focus of the current version is on exploring the functionality needed by an interactive compiler. Adding the many "bells and whistles" needed for an easy-to-learn tool will come later.

3   iCetus System Overview

The iCetus tool is implemented as a dynamic web application, generating the pages/data in real time, as per the user's request. The response will trigger from the server end and reach the client, causing the desired action. Figure 4, on page 9, illustrates this process.

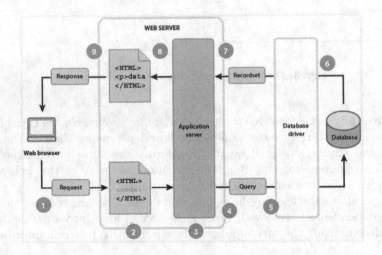

Fig. 4. Processing dynamic web pages

1. Web browser requests dynamic page.
2. Web server finds page and passes it to application server.
3. Application server scans page for instructions.
4. Application server sends query to database driver.
5. Driver executes the query against the database.
6. Record set is returned to driver.
7. Driver passes record set to application server.
8. Application server inserts data in page, and then passes the page to the web server.
9. Web server sends finished page to requesting browser.

As illustrated in Fig. 4, the current design includes a database that saves user inquiries. This information will be used for the purpose of evaluating the project.

Since the application server cannot communicate directly with the database, due to its proprietary format, an intermediary driver acts as an interpreter between the application server and the database. After the driver establishes communication, the query is executed against the database, creating a record set – a set of data extracted from one or more tables. This record set is returned to the application server to complete the page. The final result is in pure HTML format, which the application server passes back to the web server. The page is then sent to the requesting browser.

Technologies and programming languages used in developing these web pages are: JSP 2.2, Apache Tomcat version 9.0.41, JSTL 1.2, Servlet API 3, Mysql connector 8.0, OpenMp 3, Java 11.0.2, GCC 9.2.0, JavaScript 1.0, HTML 5.0, CSS 2.0.

For software design, we have used an MVC (Model-View-Controller) design pattern to separate application concerns. In this method, *Model* represents objects carrying data, *View* represents the visualization of the data, and the *Controller* acts on both model and view by controlling the data flow into model objects and updating the view whenever data changes.

4   Evaluation

To evaluate the preliminary results of the project we presented the tool to more than 20 users with different skill levels with regard to parallelization techniques and familiarity with the OpenMP parallel programming language. Our goal is to make a tool that can serve users with different skill levels that's why the feedback of all participants matters to us.

The respondents to the survey include users with diverse skill levels. 38.1% of participants are categorized as for beginners with regard to knowing parallelization techniques. 47.6% of them are categorized as intermediate having some knowledge with regard to parallelization techniques, and 14.3% of the participants are categorized as advanced being able to parallelize the code manually.

Of our participants, 66.7% of them were not familiar with OpenMP parallel programming model, while 33.3% had a good understanding of it.

We also inquired our participants about their level of familiarity with the Cetus compiler. 61.9% of users did not know the Cetus compiler but 38.1% of the participants have already tried it at least once.

We presented the list of current iCetus features and also features that we consider implementing in the next version of the tool. We asked the users to rate these features on a scale from 1 to 5, where 1 means the feature is unimportant and 5 means the feature is judged very important. We also asked for a list of features the users wish to see in such an interactive tool.

Section 4.1 shows the resulting importance of current features of the iCetus tool, Sect. 4.2 evaluates the importance of features proposed by us to be considered for the next version of the tool, and Sect. 4.3 describes the features requested by users for the next release of the project.

4.1   Importance and Usefulness of Existing iCetus Features

Figure 5, on page 11, shows the results collected on the existing features of iCetus. The user scores for all questions are above 4, indicating importance and usefulness of all implemented features.

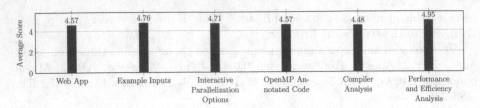

Fig. 5. User feedback on existing features

- **Web Application:** This question asked about the usefulness of iCetus being available as a web application. Having the tool implemented as a web application eliminates the need for download, install, and updates, and would be light weight on the client-side considering the fact that all the processing is done on the server-side. The high score of 4.57 indicates strong agreement with these advantages.
- **Example Inputs:** iCetus offers many example input programs that the user can choose from, illustrating key concepts of parallel programming, and transformations, as well as the tool functionalities. Users gave this feature the high score of 4.76.
- **Interactive Parallelization Options:** Users can choose parallelization options in a menu-driven way. This feature enables skilled users to take detailed control of the applied analyses and transformation techniques, while providing reasonable defaults for beginners. This question obtained a 4.71 score.
- **OpenMP Annotated Code:** Building on the Cetus source-to-source restructurer, iCetus shows the result of its transformations in the form of OpenMP-annotated source code. Users scored this feature 4.57. They also offered the following comments to explain the relevance of this capability: OpenMP-annotated source code makes it easy to understand the transformations applied to a code. The portability of OpenMP provides for a good abstraction of possible underlying machines, eliminating the need for understanding many architectural details. Similarly, reasonable performance portability is appreciated. Last but not least, the users valued the incremental parallelization process supported by this feature.
- **Compiler Analysis:** This key feature enables users to understand the applied compiler passes and inspect specific categories of program analysis results. In this way, users can query the compiler's reasoning, drilling down into questions why certain program optimizations could or could not be applied, and determining possible manual program changes to increase performance. The score for this feature was also 4.48.
- **Performance & Efficiency Analysis:** With the highest score of 4.95, users judged the availability of run-time information, such as performance and efficiency as most important. This result is consistent with the fact that the lack of run-time information can be viewed as the Achilles heel of static, batch-oriented automatic parallelization. It also points to an opportunity for

improving parallelization environments further by including additional types of dynamic program information.

4.2   Importance and Usefulness of our Proposed iCetus Features

We asked for user feedback on the features we proposed to be added to the next version of the tool. Figure 6 reports the obtained scores.

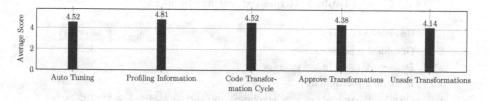

Fig. 6. User feedback on our proposed features

- **Auto-tuning:** Having an *auto-tuning* capability that determines the best combination of compiler options, obtained a score of 4.52. Some users wanted the tool to find the combination that leads to the best performance, but wanted some control over the techniques being tuned. Having such control is important, as auto-tuning can be a highly time-consuming process. Another reason given was that auto-tuning can help users learn and understand code parallelization, how it applies in different use cases, and what performance can be expected.
- **Profiling Information:** Providing loop-by-loop profiling information in the serial code and parallel code, as well as loop speedups and efficiencies, are important aids in the optimization process, indicated by the score of 4.81. The feature helps users focus attention on relevant code sections and understand performance bottlenecks.
- **Code Transformation Cycle:** Being able to modify the input code and submit it for another round of compilation is essential in an interactive optimization scenario. Applying such modifications in the presence of the available analyses information goes substantially beyond the features offered by a standard program editor. The user score for this feature was 4.52.
- **Approve Transformations:** Giving the user the ability to approve or reject transformations suggested by the parallelizer provides fine control over the code optimization process, especially for judging the profitability of a transformation. The score for this feature was 4.38.
- **Unsafe Transformations:** With a score of 4.14 users judged the importance of a capability to choose from potentially applicable transformations, even if they may be unsafe. Some users requested that this option be only available to advanced skill levels, as program correctness is no longer guaranteed.

While all scores of proposed features are above 4, they are slightly lower than those of the implemented capabilities. It can be attributed to the fact that it is easier to understand and judge existing versus projected functionality. The scores are expected to be higher, once the proposed features are implemented.

4.3   Requested Features for iCetus

One of the questions in the user interviews asked for additional suggested features. Below is the result, including the percentage of users who requested those features. The priority of implementing each feature will be based on the score. Table 1 lists these suggestions.

Table 1. Requested features by users

Row	Requested features	Priority
1	Graphical representations	33%
2	Downloading optimization reports	28%
3	Uploading multiple files	19%
4	Display differences between the input and the parallelized code	19%

- **Graphical Representations:** 33% of users requested combining text reports on the result of compiler analyses with graphical reports wherever possible.
- **Downloading Optimization Reports:** Providing the possibility of downloading the parallel code as well as the report of the compiler analyses was requested by 28% of the users.
- **Uploading Multiple Files:** 19% of users requested adding the feature to upload as many files as needed to the web server at once.
- **Display Differences Between the Input & the Parallelized Code:** 19% of users requested that the differences between the given input and the parallelized code be displayed. Such a capability would help the developer further understand the specifics of the applied code transformations.

5   Related Work

Various tools have been built in the past which aim to parallelize the sequential code. ParTool [5], which is built over the ROSE compiler infrastructure [7], inserts OpenMP pragmas in serial code. It performs data dependence analysis provided by ROSE to ascertain whether a loop nest is safe to parallelize. If not, the dependences that prevent parallelization are displayed. This feedback helps understand the dependences hindering parallelism and can be used to make suitable modifications to the source code to eliminate these dependences.

The Parascope parallelization environment [1] provides an editor that supports multiple views and navigation between views. It displays the results of the various analyses and transformations carried out by the parallelizer and binds them with the various representations used. It supports applications written in Fortran. Users have found the data dependence information to be too low-level, and they need guidance with program transforms.

HTGviz is an interactive parallelization environment. It is implemented on top of the Parafrase-2 parallelizing compiler [6]. It supports several views to the user such as, Task Graph View, Serial Code View, Directive View to insert OpenMP tags, Parallel Code View. The interaction between the user and the compiler is carried out through the use of the Hierarchical Task Graph (HTG) program representation where task parallelism is represented by precedence relations (arcs) among task nodes. There is no support for measuring the parallelization benefits, or for displaying potential parallelism, at a regional level [3].

The SUIF Explorer [4] builds on the functionality of the SUIF compiler [8] and offers assistance for both automated and manual parallel programs creation. The SUIF Explorer offers support for user visualization and provides features such as a Parallelization Guru that offers tips for parallelization, user involvement in parallel slice creation, Execution Analyzers targeting loops and dependences, Visualizers such as graph browsers and source display, and Assertion Checkers to help users debug the parallel program.

iCetus distinguishes itself from these previous efforts mainly in three ways.

- Building on one of the most advanced parallelizers, the tool allows the user to inspect in detail the result of different compiler analyses, such as data dependence analysis, variable range analysis, private variable analysis, in an easy to understand format.
- The tool provides the user with dynamic program information, such as the speedup gained from a transformation, enabling the user to judge when further optimizations may be beneficial or have diminishing return.
- The tool supports the user in all phases of the program optimization process, including profiling, parallelizing, and optimizing.

6   Conclusion

State-of-the-art parallelizing compilers are batch-oriented tools, limited to static program analyses and transformation. This paper presented the early results of a project to develop a tool that overcomes this limitation. iCetus is an effort to involve the user in the code transformation process, supporting several program development phases. A profiler helps the programmer *analyze* the code by identifying execution bottlenecks of the program. The programmer then *parallelizes* the code by starting with the most time consuming code sections while focusing on maintaining the correct results of the parallel program. *Optimizing* the code for improving observed speed-up from parallelization is the final phase. The next release of the tool will incorporate more features in support of interactivity as well as features such as a loop-level profiler, auto-tuner, and a capability to highlight differences between source and transformed code.

References

1. Balasundaram, V., Kennedy, K., Kremer, U., McKinley, K., Subhlok, J.: The paras-cope editor: an interactive parallel programming tool. In: Proceedings of the 1989 ACM/IEEE Conference on Supercomputing, Supercomputing 1989, pp. 540–550 (1989). https://doi.org/10.1145/76263.76323
2. Dave, C., Bae, H., Min, S.J., Lee, S., Eigenmann, R., Midkiff, S.: Cetus: a source-to-source compiler infrastructure for multicores. Computer **42**(12), 36–42 (2009). https://doi.org/10.1109/MC.2009.385
3. Giordano, M., Furnari, M.M.: HTGVIZ: a graphic tool for the synthesis of auto-matic and user-driven program parallelization in the compilation process. In: Poly-chronopoulos, C., Fukuda, K.J.A., Tomita, S. (eds.) ISHPC 1999. LNCS, vol. 1615, pp. 312–319. Springer, Heidelberg (1999). https://doi.org/10.1007/BFb0094932
4. Liao, S.W., Diwan, A., Bosch, R.P., Ghuloum, A., Lam, M.S.: SUIF Explorer: an interactive and interprocedural parallelizer. ACM SIGPLAN Not. **34**(8), 37–48 (1999). https://doi.org/10.1145/329366.301108
5. Mishra, V., Aggarwal, S.K.: ParTool: a feedback-directed parallelizer. In: Temam, O., Yew, P.-C., Zang, B. (eds.) APPT 2011. LNCS, vol. 6965, pp. 157–171. Springer, Heidelberg (2011). https://doi.org/10.1007/978-3-642-24151-2_12
6. Polychronopoulos, C.D., Girkar, M.B., Haghighat, M.R., Lee, C.L., Leung, B., Schouten, D.: PARAFRASE-2: an environment for parallelizing, partitioning, syn-chronizing, and scheduling programs on multiprocessors. Int. J. High Speed Comput. **01**(01), 45–72 (1989). https://doi.org/10.1142/S0129053389000044
7. Quinlan, D., Liao, C.: The ROSE source-to-source compiler infrastructure. In: Cetus Users and Compiler Infrastructure Workshop, in conjunction with PACT 2011, p. 1. Citeseer (2011)
8. Wilson, R.P., et al.: The SUIF compiler system: a parallelizing and optimizing research compiler. ACM SIGPLAN Not. (1994)

Hybrid Register Allocation with Spill Cost and Pattern Guided Optimization

Yongwon Shin and Hyojin Sung[✉]

Pohang University of Science and Technology (POSTECH), Pohang, South Korea
{ywshin,hsung}@postech.ac.kr

Abstract. Modern compilers have relied on various best-effort heuristics to solve the register allocation problem due to its high computation complexity. A "greedy" algorithm that performs a scan of prioritized live intervals for allocation followed by interval splits and spills is one of the widely used register allocation mechanisms with consistent performance and low compile-time overheads. However, its live interval splitting heuristics suffer from making sub-optimal decisions for scenarios hard to predict, and recent effort to remedy the issue is not free from unintended side effects with performance degradation. In this paper, we propose Greedy-SO, a greedy register allocator with a spill cost and pattern guided optimization that systematically addresses inherent sub-optimalities in live-interval splitting. Greedy-SO does this by avoiding splitting codes whose performance are more likely to be impacted by sub-optimal decisions. Greedy-SO identifies functions with such code patterns, precisely models the spill cost for them during the greedy allocation process, then when the spill cost starts to deteriorate, switches to an alternative allocator that does not use interval splitting. Our hybrid register allocator improves the performance of target benchmarks up to 16.1% (7.3% on average) with a low compilation overhead, while not impacting non-target benchmarks at all.

1 Introduction

Registers are scarce and valuable hardware resources whose software-managed utilization can significantly impact code performance. Modern compilers have solved the problem of register allocation, i.e., mapping infinite registers to limited architectural registers, by finding an optimal solution that maximizes utilization and minimizes memory spills [6,14]. However, the task of finding an optimal register allocation for realistic codes is an NP-complete problem [11], so various best-effort heuristics have been proposed, including graph-coloring based algorithms [8,9], linear scan algorithms [22], and their many variants [17,26]. Graph-coloring based algorithms use k-coloring heuristics to assign colors, i.e., registers, to conflicting live intervals that are represented as connected graph nodes, whereas priority-based algorithms exploit program information to determine the allocation order.

Register allocators in modern compilers implement a version of the above allocation algorithm(s) with several other heuristics when making register spill

© Springer Nature Switzerland AG 2022
X. Li and S. Chandrasekaran (Eds.): LCPC 2021, LNCS 13181, pp. 33–49, 2022.
https://doi.org/10.1007/978-3-030-99372-6_3

and live interval coalescing/splitting decisions. For example, the "greedy" algorithm in the LLVM compiler coalesces live intervals first to reduce conflicts, and allocates registers for them in their priorities computed from variable types and access patterns. Then it splits remaining unassigned intervals into pieces and spills occupied registers until the allocation is completed.

These heuristics are carefully designed and fine-tuned with expert knowledge and benchmark testing, but they are bound to suboptimal decisions due to approximate modeling of the problem. Especially the live interval splitting heuristic involves complicated logic to determine which live interval to split and where in an interval as well, which can lead to widely varying code and thus execution time. Recent work [27] tried to improve the heuristic, but it introduces performance degradation in unintended cases as a result of unpredictable chains of interactions between the changed heuristic and the rest of the register allocator.

Our insight is that problem is not the heuristic itself, but the way register allocation is performed *without* a systematic cost model that estimates the profitability of given heuristics for the code and adaptively selects allocation approaches. While previous work [10,16] enabled hybrid allocation using different allocators per function or code segment, we focus mainly on structuring *the internal phases of the allocation process* to use optimal heuristics based on modeled cost. This cost-guided optimization will enable more effective register allocation while minimizing heuristic-engineering effort and negative performance impact.

Thus, we propose Greedy-SO (**S**plit **O**ptimization), a hybrid register allocator with spill cost and pattern guided optimization for live-interval splitting logic in the LLVM greedy allocator. Our allocator uses improved spill cost modeling to detect whether and when suboptimal splitting decisions occur in the greedy allocator. Then, it switches to an alternative register allocator to finish the rest of the allocation process without splitting. We use empirically identified code patterns and thresholds to determine whether this alternative allocation path will provide performance gains and apply the path only when it is predicted to do so. The target code patterns turn out to have heavy computation in large loop bodies; this observation supports our assumption that such codes with high register pressure are more likely to suffer from the suboptimal splitting logic and benefit from our solution.

The evaluation showed that Greedy-SO improves the execution times of five benchmarks in LLVM test suite by 7.3% on average (up to 16.1%) *without degrading other benchmarks* on Intel CPU. These benchmarks can be used as building blocks for larger applications, so the potential performance gain will be significant at an application level. We believe that this paper demonstrates the promising potential towards optimization-driven back-end code generation.

In the rest of the paper, motivating insights and preliminary analysis are presented in Sects. 2 and 3. Then we describe the design and implementation of Greedy-SO in detail in Sect. 4. We describe the experimental setup for Greedy-SO and other allocators in Sect. 5 and give results in Sect. 6, then conclude with related work and a conclusion.

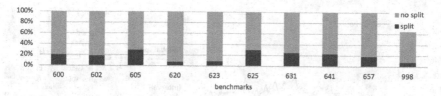

Fig. 1. The ratio of functions entering the split phase in SPEC2017 intspeed

2 Background and Challenges

We made the following observations that reveal the challenges of existing register allocators that guided our design in Sects. 3 and 4.

Observation 1. Codes compiled with the greedy allocator are subject to high performance variability from live interval splitting heuristics. The LLVM greedy register allocator consists of three main phases. As a preliminary step, it computes live intervals of virtual registers and assigns priorities by using program-based criteria, e.g., giving a higher priority to global variables and variables within a loop. The coalescing phase combines related live intervals by making copies to reduce register pressure. During the allocation phase, the live intervals sorted in a priority queue are assigned to an available register. The register allocation may finish here if no registers remain to be allocated, or may move on to the final split/spill phase, which splits allocated live intervals into smaller ones to reassign them or spills live intervals to the memory to make room.

All the heuristics in these phases interact closely to generate final allocation, and attempts to precisely analyze its workings are likely to be fruitless. However, we observe that the live interval splitting heuristics have a much larger decision space than the others, e.g., whether to split or spill, which live interval to split, where in a live interval to split and at which level (region, block, or local), and in how many sub-intervals to create, which can lead to higher performance variability caused by heuristic design. Considering the fact that more than 25% of the functions in SPEC2017 must go through the split/spill phase when compiled with default options for Intel CPU (Fig. 1), optimizing the heuristics in the split/spill phase can yield performance gain for a wide range of codes on dominant CPU platforms.

Observation 2. Optimizing heuristics for specific cases often introduces unexpected performance degradation in others. Carefully designed heuristics are often updated to handle corner cases that perform pathologically badly under different circumstances. However, once heuristics are mature, adjusting them to fix specific cases without negative side effects is very difficult and requires significant engineering and testing effort without a guarantee of success. For example, recent work [27] identified and addressed the issue of not considering local interference as weights in the region-level splitting heuristic. Although it works well for target testcases, it randomly introduces runtime slow-down, because the changed heuristic can cause unexpected side effects with the rest of the register

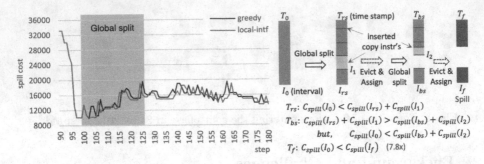

Fig. 2. Cost tracking graph (left) and a case of suboptimal splitting (right) for bicubic interpolation kernel [4]. The orange box in the left indicates where region and block splits happen. (Color figure online)

allocator as reported by the community and our evaluation. This observation calls for detailed cost modeling of the heuristics to reveal potential suboptimal decisions and adaptively apply optimizations based on cost prediction.

3   Preliminary Analysis

To understand how heuristic decisions affect the potential cost of register allocation, we modeled the register spill cost for each live interval as follows:

$$C_{load} = \sum_{u \in U} B_{freq}(u), \; C_{save} = B_{freq}(d) \tag{1}$$

$$C_{spill} = R * (C_{load} + C_{save}) \tag{2}$$

$$C_{total\_spill} = \sum_{i \in I} C_{spill}(i) \tag{3}$$

where B_{freq} is block frequency and $0 \leq R \leq 1$ is a rematerialization ratio.

C_{load} and C_{save} estimate runtime memory load and save costs by summing up block frequencies for each use (u) and definition (d) in a given live interval. A live interval in LLVM is defined per virtual register, for which (d) is unique per interval in the SSA form [23]. C_{spill} is computed as a sum of the two costs discounted by R (=0.5 if all uses are rematerializable). By summing C_{spill} of the spilled intervals and that of intervals in the priority queue, C_{total_spill} conservatively estimates the memory spill cost of the current register allocation state assuming the worse cases in which all remaining intervals are spilled.

Similar forms of spill costs have been used to evaluate the efficiency of register allocators in prior work [8,24], but they focus on computing the final spill cost after register allocation has been completed. We designed this spill cost to estimate the cost of register-to-memory spills at a given point of the register allocation process. This spill cost is also different from the weight used in the greedy allocator for many heuristic decisions including splits and spills. The greedy allocator normalizes the weight with live-interval length so that it can prefer short live intervals for allocation and long live intervals for splitting [21]. We do not factor live interval lengths into our spill cost because it is designed to keep track of "after-the-fact" states of a heuristic decision.

No live intervals are assigned yet at the beginning of register allocation, so we start at the highest possible spill cost assuming that they will be all spilled into the memory and should be loaded to registers for execution. As live intervals are allocated to registers, the spill cost decreases. Live interval splitting will increase the spill cost by the sum of block frequency for each inserted instruction, then decrease it by assigning a split live interval to a register. Register spills increase the spill cost by the cost of the live interval.

Ideally, the spill cost should decrease continuously throughout the register allocation process, producing the minimal cost at the end. Splits create spikes but the spill cost after a split should be lower than before. However, our preliminary experiments with LLVM test suite benchmarks reveal many non-ideal cases. The final spill costs obtained by the original greedy allocator and an optimized version [27] are both higher than the minimal cost obtained early in the split phase (Fig. 2). A closer look at a suboptimal splitting case as shown on the right side of Fig. 2 reveals that the final spill cost at T_f ends up higher than the spill cost before splits at T_0. Split attempts at T_{rs} and T_{bs} allow I_1 and I_2 to be allocated and thereby reduce the total cost, but the costs of inserting copy instructions are higher than this reduction. This suboptimal behavior is challenging to predict with iterative eviction-assignment chains. Our preliminary analysis revealed the following.

1. The *global-split* heuristic, which considers live intervals that span multiple basic blocks for splitting candidates, makes suboptimal decisions, thus causing the overall spill cost to increase after a split. This issue is partially addressed by [27].
2. Cost tracking graphs for many benchmarks show suboptimalities with the *block-split* heuristic as well. This result occurs because the current greedy allocator does not consider the local interference for block splitting, and the issue has not been reported or addressed by prior work.
3. [27] can make different suboptimal decisions than the baseline greedy allocator leading to an even higher spill cost at the end, and thus worse performance (details in Sect. 6). This result shows that [27] cannot be trusted to improve the allocation quality in general.

The analysis result, combined with the observations in Sect. 2, guides our systematic cost-driven design of register allocator in the next section that focuses on addressing suboptimalities at an allocation strategy level rather than an individual heuristic design level.

4   Design and Implementation

Figure 3 shows the compilation flow of the Greedy-SO register allocator with three main components. It consists of two cost models, **code pattern recognizer** and **spill cost tracking mechanism**, and **cost-guided allocation**

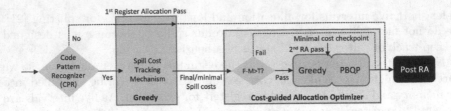

Fig. 3. The overview of Greedy-SO

optimizer that selectively applies hybrid register allocation based on the combined cost. The code pattern recognizer (CPR) serves as a counter-based filter to determine whether the compiled code is an optimization candidate that requires detailed spill cost tracking. Second, for identified candidates, the spill cost tracking mechanism computes the spill cost as proposed in Sect. 3 during register allocation to detect potential suboptimalities. The two costs, i.e., code statistics and spill cost, are evaluated sequentially to eliminate spill cost tracking overheads for non-target codes. Lastly, after the first register allocation process, the cost-guided allocation optimizer examines the minimum spill cost (M) and the final spill cost (F) with a threshold (T), and if the condition is met, reverts the allocation result and executes an alternative allocation path from when the minimal spill cost is reached. The following sections describe the design and implementation of each component in detail.

4.1   Code Pattern Recognizer

The code pattern recognizer (CPR) collects counter-based code statistics by recursively traversing all loops in a function and computing conditions that represent the target code pattern of the Greedy-SO register allocator. The goal of the CPR is to focus on optimizing functions for which suboptimal splits are likely to be translated into performance gains; i.e., it filters out functions that are too sensitive to architectural noises such as code alignment and instruction cache misses [2]. For example, we observed that when most of the innermost loops are small or instructions in small inner loops dominate the total number of instructions, non-deterministic side effects caused by changes in register allocation often hide the performance benefit of Greedy-SO. Thus, CPR checks if any of the following conditions holds for filtering.

1. Small loops only. CPR filters out functions in which basic blocks in loops all have less than $C_{small} (= 10)$ instructions. While small loops can go through the split/spill phase, they are susceptible to microarchitectural noises and not likely to have stable performance gains from our optimization.

$$F_{small\_loop} = \begin{cases} true & \text{if all basic blocks has less than } C_{small} \text{ instructions} \\ & \text{in all loops} \\ false & \text{otherwise} \end{cases} \quad (4)$$

2. Many small innermost loops. CPR applies relaxed filtering criteria with an increased threshold for $C_{small} (= 15)$ and tries to detect functions that have many innermost loops whose majority are small. This condition targets functions with many function calls inlined by small loops.

$$F_{small\_inline} = \begin{cases} true & \text{if } (L_{inner} > c_1) \wedge (ratio\_small > c_2) \\ false & \text{otherwise} \end{cases} \tag{5}$$

where $ratio\_small = L_{small\_inner}/L_{inner}, c_1 = 30, c_2 = 0.85$.

3. Middle-sized loops. CPR further relaxes the criteria to detect middle-sized loops, by decreasing the $ratio\_small$ threshold. We observed that even when $ratio\_small$ is moderately high, if a function also has many instructions in non-small and non-innermost loop bodies, then Greedy-SO can tolerate architectural performance jitters. This condition is checked by comparing the ratio of I_{middle_loop} (# of instructions in non-innermost or non-small loops) and I_{inner} (# of instructions in small innermost loops).

$$f_1 = \begin{cases} true & \text{if } (ratio\_small > c_3) \wedge (I_{middle\_loop} < I_{inner} * c_4) \\ false & \text{otherwise} \end{cases} \tag{6}$$

$$f_2 = \begin{cases} true & \text{if } (ratio\_small > c_5) \wedge (I_{middle\_loop} < I_{inner} * c_6) \\ false & \text{otherwise} \end{cases} \tag{7}$$

$$F_{middle\_loop} = f_1 \vee f_2 \tag{8}$$

where f_1 uses $c_3 = 0.5$ and $c_4 = 3.5$ while f_2 uses more relaxed parameters than f_1: $c_5 = 0.4$ and $c_6 = 4.2$.

Finally, CPR filters out a function if any of the previous conditions is true.

$$F = F_{small\_loop} \vee F_{small\_inline} \vee F_{middle\_loop} \tag{9}$$

The filtering conditions and parameters(C_{small}, c_1 to c_6) were hand-tuned using results of experiments on Intel and AMD machines. Adopting a more systematic and learning-based approach such as rule induction [13] can help improve the heuristic design, and it is part of our future work.

Figure 4 shows examples of target and non-target functions. The function on the left has an innermost loop that includes many array accesses on distinct locations (in red). This function must perform numerous live interval splits and spills due to high register pressure. Also, improved register allocation for the large inner loops will have high performance impact. In contrast, the function on the right has only one loop nest with a small innermost loop (in green). Even if the spill cost modeling reveals suboptimalities, non-deterministic architectural behaviors could easily offset performance gain by Greedy-SO.

4.2 Spill Cost Tracking Mechanism

We implemented the spill code computation and tracking in the LLVM greedy allocator as described in Sect. 3. C_{spill} is computed for every live interval when

```
float jacobi(...) {...                          int dfilter(...) ... {
for(n=0 ; n<nn ; n++){                             ...
  gosa = 0.0;                                       for (i=0; i<high; i++)
  for(i=1 ; i<imax; i++)                              for (j=0; j<larg; j++) {
    for(j=1 ; j<jmax ; j++)                             for (l=-(tm_g/2); l<=(tm_g/2); l++) {
      for(k=1 ; k<kmax ; k++) {              if ((j+l) < 0) nv = (float) image[i*larg];
    s0= MR(a,0,i,j,k)*MR(p,0,i+1,j,  k)       else if ((j+l) >= larg) nv = (float) image[((i+1)*larg)-1];
       + MR(a,1,i,j,k)*MR(p,0,i,  j+1,k)      else nv = (float) image[(i*larg)+j+1];
       + MR(a,2,i,j,k)*MR(p,0,i,  j,  k+1)    *d = (nv * g[(tm_g/2)-1]) + *d;
       + MR(b,0,i,j,k)                                }
       *( MR(p,0,i+1,j+1,k) - MR(p,0,i+1,j-1,k)        d++;
        - MR(p,0,i-1,j+1,k) + MR(p,0,i-1,j-1,k) )   }
       + MR(b,1,i,j,k)
       *( MR(p,0,i,j+1,k+1) - MR(p,0,i,j-1,k+1)    ...
        - MR(p,0,i,j+1,k-1) + MR(p,0,i,j-1,k-1) )   d2 = (float *) calloc(nc*nr, FWS);
       + MR(b,2,i,j,k)                             if (!d2) {
       *( MR(p,0,i+1,j,k+1) - MR(p,0,i-1,j,k+1)       sprintf(err,"Out of memory");
        - MR(p,0,i+1,j,k-1) + MR(p,0,i-1,j,k-1) )     return(1);
       + MR(c,0,i,j,k) * MR(p,0,i-1,j,  k)        }
       + MR(c,1,i,j,k) * MR(p,0,i,  j-1,k)        ···     ▲ Non-target function with low register pressure in the loop
       + MR(c,2,i,j,k) * MR(p,0,i,  j,  k-1)
       + MR(wrk1,0,i,j,k);                    ◀ Target function of high register pressure and local interferences in the loop
  ... }
```

Fig. 4. Example target and non-target functions for Greedy-SO (Color figure online)

created and pushed into a priority queue, then recomputed when a new interval is generated by live interval splitting. C_{total_spill} is computed at the following tracking points in the register allocation process: (1) when a live interval is enqueued into the priority queue, (2) when a live interval is dequeued from the priority queue, and (3) when a spill occurs.

For example, when a split happens, an interval is dequeued from the priority queue at t_0 and split into smaller intervals. The total spill cost does not change for the dequeue action, because we conservatively count intervals in the queue as potential spills. Then the split intervals are enqueued back to the priority queue for allocation at t_1. At this point, the total cost will go up as a split introduces additional copy instructions at interval boundaries. When split intervals are dequeued and allocated later at t_2, a successful allocation will eventually result in a lower spill cost than the spill cost at t_0 as their costs are all deducted from the total spill cost. However, suboptimal splitting decisions that cause spills for split intervals will not be able to deduct their costs, so the total spill cost will stay higher than the cost at t_0. The key idea behind Greedy-SO is that if the total spill cost gets much worse after reaching the minimum early in the process, stopping when the minimum is reached can avoid suboptimal splitting decisions afterward.

We keep track of the minimal total spill cost by comparing a newly computed total spill cost with the current minimal total spill cost at the above tracking points, then make a checkpoint for when a new minimum appears. A checkpoint is stored as the number of "dequeue" events of the priority queue. Greedy-SO uses this checkpoint to determine when an alternate fall-back allocator takes over the allocation process.

4.3   Putting it all Together: Cost-Guided Allocation Optimizer

After the first register allocation with the spill cost tracking enabled, the cost-guided allocation optimizer compares the final spill cost ($cost_f$) and the minimum spill cost ($cost_m$) and evaluates the following condition to decide whether or not to proceed to hybrid register allocation:

$$(cost_f \geq 100 \ \wedge \ cost_m < cost_f * 0.9) \ \vee$$
$$(50 \leq cost_f < 100 \ \wedge \ cost_m < cost_f * 0.8) \tag{10}$$

The condition filter outs codes with a spill cost lower than 50 since such functions should be very small and not worth optimizing. Conversely, the condition favors codes with a high spill cost (>100) which are likely to have a high performance impact by giving them a weak threshold. A function that passes this test is recognized as a target function of Greedy-SO optimization.

Then Greedy-SO starts the second register allocation pass as the greedy allocator using a snapshot of machine functions created before the first allocation pass (details in Sect. 5). When Greedy-SO arrives at the saved checkpoint, it passes the analysis result and current allocation information to a fall-back register allocator, Partitioned Boolean Quadratic Programming (PBQP) [18,25] or to an LLVM Basic allocator. PBQP constructs a cost matrix for each pair of virtual registers and records spill cost, register aliasing information, and optional coalescing profitability. Then it tries a PBQP solver to get a solution. If a solution is not found, registers with the lowest spill cost are spilled, and the PBQP allocator repeats the process until all the constraints are satisfied. Greedy-SO passes a pointer to LLVM spiller (in charge of register spills) to PBQP. Once PBQP takes over, it solves the remaining allocation problem from the checkpoint.

5   Methodology

Compiler Implementation. We implemented Greedy-SO in LLVM 13 [19] by modifying the greedy register allocator to follow the compilation flow of Greedy-SO when a compilation option "use-greedy-so" is given. If a function is identified as a target function after the first allocation pass, a modified `FPPassManager` clones the original function at LLVM IR level and replaces all uses of the target function with those of the cloned function. Then, the cloned function goes through the same machine function passes as the original function, then through the Greedy-SO register allocation pass.

Benchmarks. For experimental results, we evaluated 737 benchmarks from the LLVM test suite [3] except for the ones under "External" and "CTMark" categories, with a testing option (`TEST_SUITE_BENCHMARKING_ONLY`). Experiments were repeated ten times with a single thread and default inputs using `llvm-lit` test tool.

Experimental Setup. For Greedy-SO, we used 0.1 as the minimal spill cost threshold to trigger hybrid register allocation (i.e., the difference between the minimal spill cost and the final spill cost should be higher than 10%), and used a PBQP register allocator in LLVM whose implementation is based on [18]. We performed a sensitivity study (Sect. 6.2) to see how the spill cost threshold and the type of fall-back register allocator affect the performance of Greedy-SO. The evaluated configurations are as follows:

- *greedy* and *pbqp*: The original LLVM greedy and PBQP allocator in LLVM 13 with default options.
- *local-intf*: *greedy* with "consider-local-interval-cost" option enabled [27].
- *gs* and *gs-basic*: *gs* is Greedy-SO, and *gs-basic* replaces the fall-back register allocator with the LLVM basic register allocator.
- *gs-wop-pbqp*, *gs-wop-pbqp-0.1* and *gs-wop-pbqp-0.2*: Greedy-SO without the code pattern recognizer with varying spill cost threshold. *gs-wop-pbqp* has 0 for the threshold, i.e., it always triggers hybrid register allocation when the final spill cost is not the minimal spill cost, while 0.1 and 0.2 signify the required difference ratios between minimum spill cost and final spill cost for the trigger.
- *gs-wop-basic*, *gs-wop-basic-0.1* and *gs-wop-basic-0.2*: *gs-basic* without the code pattern recognizer with varying spill cost thresholds.

We evaluated LLVM test suite on Intel (Xeon Gold 5218 CPU with 375 GB RAM), AMD (EPYC 7571 with 64 GB RAM), and ARM (Neoverse N1 with 64 GB RAM) CPU platforms. Hyperthreading and CPU frequency scaling were disabled for the Intel CPU.

6   Evaluation Result

In our evaluation of the Greedy-SO register allocator, we focus on showing that Greedy-SO provides improved or comparable performance to the greedy allocator, for target codes identified by the cost models. We also compared Greedy-SO with previous work [27] and variations of Greedy-SO to show that both the spill cost modeling and pattern-based filtering are crucial to provide consistent speedup without degradation.

6.1   Benchmark Performance

Execution times were evaluated (Figs. 5 and 6) for a set of LLVM test suite benchmarks (Table 1), normalized to LLVM greedy allocator. We evaluated the entire test suite with these allocators and found out that 97.7% (97.8% in AMD) of the total benchmarks show less than 2% of performance variations regardless of the type of register allocator. While 2.3% (2.2% in AMD) of such benchmarks include target functions for Greedy-SO optimization, most of them have a negligible performance impact. Thus, we focus on investigating the benchmarks whose execution time is affected by more than 2% in either direction, with any of the

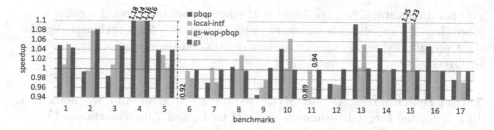

Fig. 5. Execution times of LLVM test suite on Intel CPU (normalized to *greedy*)

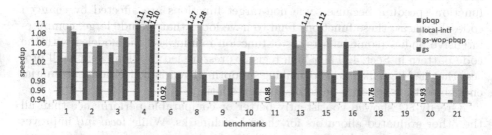

Fig. 6. Execution times of LLVM test suite on AMD CPU (normalized to *greedy*)

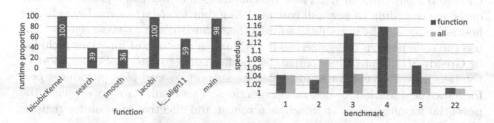

Fig. 7. Comparison of target function performance (*function*) and benchmark performance (*all*) (right) and the runtime proportion of target functions (left).

Table 1. Selected LLVM test suite benchmark list.

Benchmarks					
1	BICUCIB_INTERPOLATION	9	lencod	17	functionobjects
2	aha	10	lambda	18	MemCmp<4, EqZero, None>
3	miniGMG	11	lua	19	SIBsim4
4	himenobmtxpa	12	siod	20	obsequi
5	pairlocalalign	13	PathFinder	21	sqlite3
6	ENERGY_CALC_LAMBDA	14	XSBench	22	dynprog
7	TRAP_INT_RAW	15	yacr2		
8	FIND_FIRST_MIN_LAMBDA	16	ks		

evaluated allocators. In Figs. 5 and 6, the benchmarks in the left section show more than 2% speedup (or slowdown) with Greedy-SO; the benchmarks on the right are affected more than 2% by other evaluated register allocators, but not by Greedy-SO.

Target Benchmarks. Greedy-SO showed average speedups of 7.3% (maximum 16.1%) for the target benchmarks on Intel CPU, and 7.9% (maximum 10.1%) on AMD CPU. Function-level analysis revealed that functions optimized with Greedy-SO in these benchmarks do contribute mainly to the overall speedup, as shown in Fig. 7. For benchmark 2, the overall speedup is greater than the per-function speedup, because some non-target functions are affected by changed code alignment; these functions tend to have loops that include large, compute-intensive bodies (some as a result of function inlining) as we modeled with the code pattern in Sect. 4. Their high register pressure led to a long split/spill process that had high likelihood of making suboptimal heuristic decisions substantial enough to translate into performance degradation.

Greedy-SO showed consistently better or comparable performance than all the other evaluated allocators for these benchmarks. While *local-intf* improves on greedy for several benchmarks, it does not show any performance improvement with some of the benchmarks where Greedy-SO does (2 and 3 on Intel CPU and 2 on AMD CPU). These benchmarks suffer from suboptimal heuristic decisions according to our spill cost modeling, but *local-intf* as another splitting heuristic seems to be not able to address them consistently. *gs-wop-pbqp* does not use the code pattern recognizer, so it optimizes a superset of functions included in Greedy-SO. It provides comparable performance to Greedy-SO for most of the benchmark except for 5, for which we suspect *gs-wop-pbqp* introduces performance degradation for non-target functions. This result strongly supports the potential for our hybrid approach as a robust and effective solution for register allocation.

Although the performance gain on Intel and AMD CPU vary due to microarchitectural differences, they affect the same set of benchmarks except for 5. This result shows that the code pattern that we used can generalize across different hardware.

Non-target Benchmarks. The right section in Figs. 5 and 6 includes the benchmarks with more than 2% performance jitter with the other register allocators than Greedy-SO. We analyzed those benchmarks to quantify the effectiveness of the combination of the spill cost and code patterns in Greedy-SO in avoiding potential performance degradation by focusing on profitable cases only. Only 0.63% (0.55% in AMD) of the functions in these benchmarks are optimized by Greedy-SO while the rest does not satisfy both conditions. As a result, Greedy-SO and greedy show little performance difference.

In contrast, the execution times of the other register allocators varied without any consistent trend. For example, the execution time of *pbqp* and *local-intf* fluctuated from -24% to 28%; understanding its source is not in the scope of

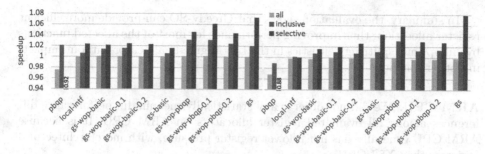

Fig. 8. Sensitivity study for spill cost thresholds and fall-back register type. *all* shows average performance for the entire LLVM test suite (737 total), while *selective* is for the subset of benchmarks with more than 2% performance difference compared the greedy allocator in a given configuration and *inclusive* is for the union of *selective* sets (except for *pbqp* sets; 25 for Intel and 26 for AMD).

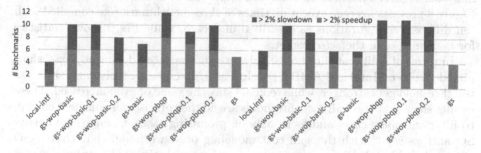

Fig. 9. Function performance of the *selective* benchmark set for configurations with different fall-back register allocators and spill cost threshold. (Color figure online)

this paper. *gs-wop-pbqp* generously applies hybrid register allocation whenever the spill cost indicates suboptimalities. This strategy produces a mixed result of improving or degrading non-target functions. We found that performance degradation is a result of random negative side effects from changed allocation being stronger than the speedup gain. We can see that the code pattern recognizer is crucial in avoiding these cases and applying the optimization only when overall speedup is expected.

As for the benchmarks with performance improvement (8, 10, 13, 14, 15 and 16), we identified two main sources. In some cases, our code pattern is too strong and restrictive to identify marginally profitable codes as target functions (details in Sect. 6.2). We also discovered that a significant speedup for 8 comes from the internal workings of microarchitectural features in Intel CPU. When a function has many small innermost loops, its execution time gets very sensitive to the code size and alignment. We excluded functions likely to trigger this phenomenon from our code pattern for the stable outcome without performance degradation.

In summary, the evaluation shows that Greedy-SO can provide more efficient register allocation, thus improving performance for most of the affected functions by suboptimal splitting heuristics in the LLVM greedy allocator without impacting other functions.

ARM CPU. We did not observe any statistically meaningful performance differences among all evaluated register allocators on ARM CPU. It is because ARM CPU generally has much lower register pressure, with more architectural registers than X86 CPU's.

6.2 Sensitivity Study

We conducted a sensitivity study with varying spill cost thresholds and types of fall-back register allocator on Intel and AMD CPU, as shown in Figs. 8 and 9. Figure 8 presents average execution times of three benchmark sets compiled with ten different configurations as described in Sect. 5, while Fig. 9 shows statistics for benchmarks in the *selective* set.

In terms of spill cost thresholds, both *gs-wop-basic-** and *gs-wop-pbqp-** show mixed results on Intel and AMD CPU. In Fig. 9, green bars consistently shrink as the threshold gets stronger, while red bars stay the same or even increased. These results show that the spill cost thresholds are neither precise nor sufficient enough to filter out noisy cases and focus only on promising cases. Comparing Greedy-SO and *gs-wop-** with the spill cost modeling only, we found that Greedy-SO efficiently excludes noisy cases than the versions with thresholds only.

Another important factor is the efficiency of the fall-back register allocator, which determines how much improvement over the existing greedy allocator can be achieved. Figure 8 shows that *gs-wop-pbqp-** and *gs* provide performance comparable to or higher than *gs-wop-basic-** and *gs-basic*. We observed that a conservative and quick eviction algorithm of the basic allocator may accidentally spill high-priority registers. In contrast, when a spill occurs, the PBQP allocator repeatedly solves the remaining allocation problem until there are no more spills, preventing bad spills caused by evictions. Comparing Greedy-SO and *gs-basic* to isolate the effect of the fall-back register allocator with the same cost models and the same target functions, Greedy-SO provides 7% and 8% speedup on Intel and AMD CPU without any performance degradation (no red bar in Fig. 9), while *gs-basic* struggles with performance degradation.

Considering the results of this sensitivity study, we used the PBQP allocator as a fall-back register allocator for Greedy-SO and a threshold of 0.1 for the Greedy-SO register allocator.

6.3 Compilation Overhead

Greedy-SO introduces the overhead of recompilation only for the functions identified by both of the cost models as shown in Fig. 3.

The overhead of performing additional Greedy-SO register allocation path including IR function cloning and reverting logic is 1.7% (1.1% in AMD) of the total compilation time for LLVM CTMark benchmarks.

Cloning function at machine function or MIR level or reverting only the register allocation result could further reduce recompilation overhead, but it is a non-trivial task [1,5] and not in the scope of the paper.

7 Related Work

Linear scan register allocators [22] have been widely adopted as a cost-efficient alternative to the graph coloring-based register allocator [8]. [24] showed that the linear scan allocator can seamlessly combine with SSA forms [20] to outperform the coloring-based algorithms, and LLVM 3.0 further improved its linear scan allocator to use priority-based allocation [12] and enable global live interval splitting. Greedy-SO focuses on solving suboptimal decisions in these splitting heuristics.

[27] identified pathological cases caused by local interference not being considered during global-split in the greedy allocator. It examines whether a region split may produce a local live interval that requires additional splits or spills due to interference and avoids splitting such candidates by boosting their potential spill cost. It improves performance for its target test cases, but can have adverse side effects as shown in our evaluation. [7] recently reported that regional interference across multiple basic blocks should also be checked if they may introduce additional spilling, but the issue has not been addressed yet. Instead of tackling issues one by one at the heuristic design level, Greedy-SO systematically exploits spill cost modeling to avoid suboptimalities at a higher level.

Some recent work has used hybrid or mixed register allocation schemes for efficiency and flexibility. [10] chooses between linear scan and graph coloring register allocators by comparing the spill costs of the two allocators to generate labels and train a rule induction model with them. Greedy-SO also uses spill cost tracking, but it builds a cost-guided optimization that integrates the two register allocators instead of choosing one or the other. It also uses a high-level code pattern recognizer for more fine-grained hybrid register allocation. [16] dynamically chooses a register allocator for small code segments called "traces" by using allocation policies based on live interval analysis, loop depth, and block frequencies. Greedy-SO is different in reusing the existing global register allocators with minimal implementation overheads, but adapting the allocation policies for Greedy-SO will be interesting future work. [15] suggested feedback-directed JIT compilation frameworks that formulate register spills as an ILP problem and make spill decisions using solutions from previous compilation. Greedy-SO currently focuses on improving the register allocator for AOT (Ahead-Of-Time) compilation with a single re-compilation.

8   Conclusion and Future Work

In this paper, we proposed Greedy-SO with the cost models for hybrid register allocation. In an effort to overcome the inherent limitations of heuristic fine-tuning, Greedy-SO provides a systematic way to detect suboptimal heuristic decisions and bypass them altogether and to do so only when performance benefit is expected. Our experiment showed that Greedy-SO could outperform the LLVM greedy allocator for target benchmarks without impacting non-target benchmarks, unlike prior work. Our future work includes extending our approach to other back-end code generation phases and introducing additional cost-guided optimization passes, targeting other CPU and GPU platforms, and modeling learned predictors for the spill cost and code patterns to reduce the compilation overhead and improve the accuracy.

Acknowledgement. This work was supported by Institute for Information & communications Technology Promotion (IITP) grants funded by the Korea government (MSIP) (No. 2019-0-01906, Artificial Intelligence Graduate School Program (POSTECH) and No. 2021-0-00310, AI Frameworks) and the Super Computer Development Leading Program of the National Research Foundation of Korea (NRF) funded by the Korean government (Ministry of Science and ICT (MSIT)) (No. 2020M3H6A1084853).

References

1. Cloning MachineFunctions. https://groups.google.com/g/llvm-dev/c/DOP6RSV8 lQ4/m/C3Lfe6gJEwAJ
2. Intel(R) 64 and IA-32 architectures optimization reference manual. https://www.intel.com/content/dam/www/public/us/en/documents/manuals/64-ia-32-architectures-optimization-manual.pdf
3. LLVM testing infrastructure. https://github.com/llvm/llvm-test-suite
4. Parallel bicubic interpolation. https://github.com/srijanmishra/parallel-bicubic-interpolation
5. Suggestions on register allocation by using reinforcement learning. https://groups.google.com/g/llvm-dev/c/V9ykDwqGeNw/m/-3SfJsuRAQAJ
6. Aho, A.V., Sethi, R., Ullman, J.D.: Compilers, Principles, Techniques, and Tools. Addison-Wesley, New York (1986)
7. Brawn, J.: Strange regalloc behaviour: one more available register causes much worse allocation, December 2018. https://lists.llvm.org/pipermail/llvm-dev/2018-December/128299.html
8. Briggs, P., Cooper, K.D., Torczon, L.: Improvements to graph coloring register allocation. ACM Trans. Program. Lang. Syst. (TOPLAS) **16**(3), 428–455 (1994)
9. Callahan, D., Koblenz, B.: Register allocation via hierarchical graph coloring. ACM Sigplan Not. **26**(6), 192–203 (1991)
10. Cavazos, J., Moss, J.E.B., O'Boyle, M.F.P.: Hybrid optimizations: which optimization algorithm to use? In: Mycroft, A., Zeller, A. (eds.) CC 2006. LNCS, vol. 3923, pp. 124–138. Springer, Heidelberg (2006). https://doi.org/10.1007/11688839_12
11. Chaitin, G.J., Auslander, M.A., Chandra, A.K., Cocke, J., Hopkins, M.E., Markstein, P.W.: Register allocation via coloring. Comput. Lang. **6**(1), 47–57 (1981)

12. Chow, F.C., Hennessy, J.L.: The priority-based coloring approach to register allocation. ACM Trans. Program. Lang. Syst. **12**(4), 501–536 (1990). https://doi.org/10.1145/88616.88621
13. Cohen, W.W.: Fast effective rule induction. In: Prieditis, A., Russell, S. (eds.) Machine Learning Proceedings 1995, pp. 115–123. Morgan Kaufmann, San Francisco (CA) (1995). https://doi.org/10.1016/B978-1-55860-377-6.50023-2, https://www.sciencedirect.com/science/article/pii/B9781558603776500232
14. Cooper, K.D., Torczon, L.: Engineering a Compiler, 2nd edn. Morgan Kaufmann, Boston (2012). https://doi.org/10.1016/B978-0-12-088478-0.00001-3, https://www.sciencedirect.com/science/article/pii/B9780120884780000013
15. Diouf, B., Cohen, A., Rastello, F., Cavazos, J.: Split register allocation: linear complexity without the performance penalty. In: Patt, Y.N., Foglia, P., Duesterwald, E., Faraboschi, P., Martorell, X. (eds.) HiPEAC 2010. LNCS, vol. 5952, pp. 66–80. Springer, Heidelberg (2010). https://doi.org/10.1007/978-3-642-11515-8_7
16. Eisl, J., Marr, S., Würthinger, T., Mössenböck, H.: Trace register allocation policies: compile-time vs. performance trade-offs. In: Proceedings of the 14th International Conference on Managed Languages and Runtimes, pp. 92–104 (2017)
17. Evlogimenos, A.: Improvements to linear scan register allocation (2004). https://llvm.org/ProjectsWithLLVM/2004-Fall-CS426-LS.pdf
18. Hames, L., Scholz, B.: Nearly optimal register allocation with PBQP. In: Lightfoot, D.E., Szyperski, C. (eds.) JMLC 2006. LNCS, vol. 4228, pp. 346–361. Springer, Heidelberg (2006). https://doi.org/10.1007/11860990_21
19. Lattner, C., Adve, V.: LLVM: a compilation framework for lifelong program analysis & transformation. In: International Symposium on Code Generation and Optimization, 2004. CGO 2004, pp. 75–86. IEEE (2004)
20. Mössenböck, H., Pfeiffer, M.: Linear scan register allocation in the context of SSA form and register constraints. In: Horspool, R.N. (ed.) CC 2002. LNCS, vol. 2304, pp. 229–246. Springer, Heidelberg (2002). https://doi.org/10.1007/3-540-45937-5_17
21. Olesen, J.S.: Greedy register allocation, September 2011. http://blog.llvm.org/2011/09/greedy-register-allocation-in-llvm-30.html
22. Poletto, M., Sarkar, V.: Linear scan register allocation. ACM Trans. Prog. Lang. Syst. (TOPLAS) **21**(5), 895–913 (1999)
23. Rosen, B.K., Wegman, M.N., Zadeck, F.K.: Global value numbers and redundant computations. In: Proceedings of the 15th ACM SIGPLAN-SIGACT Symposium on Principles of Programming Languages, pp. 12–27, POPL 1988. Association for Computing Machinery, New York, NY, USA (1988). https://doi.org/10.1145/73560.73562
24. Sarkar, V., Barik, R.: Extended linear scan: an alternate foundation for global register allocation. In: Krishnamurthi, S., Odersky, M. (eds.) CC 2007. LNCS, vol. 4420, pp. 141–155. Springer, Heidelberg (2007). https://doi.org/10.1007/978-3-540-71229-9_10
25. Scholz, B., Eckstein, E.: Register allocation for irregular architectures. In: Proceedings of the Joint Conference on Languages, Compilers and Tools for Embedded Systems: Software and Compilers for Embedded Systems, pp. 139–148 (2002)
26. Wimmer, C., Mössenböck, H.: Optimized interval splitting in a linear scan register allocator. In: Proceedings of the 1st ACM/USENIX International Conference on Virtual Execution Environments, pp. 132–141 (2005)
27. Yatsina, M.: Improving region split decisions, April 2018. https://llvm.org/devmtg/2018-04/slides/Yatsina-LLVMGreedyRegisterAllocator.pdf

Performance Evaluation of OSCAR Multi-target Automatic Parallelizing Compiler on Intel, AMD, Arm and RISC-V Multicores

Birk Martin Magnussen$^{(\boxtimes)}$ ⓘ, Tohma Kawasumi, Hiroki Mikami,
Keiji Kimura, and Hironori Kasahara

Department of Computer Science and Engineering, Waseda University, Green
Computing Center, 27 Waseda-machi, Shinjuku-ku, Tokyo 162-0042, Japan
{birk_magnussen,tohma,hiroki}@kasahara.cs.waseda.ac.jp,
{keiji,kasahara}@waseda.jp
http://www.kasahara.cs.waseda.ac.jp/index.html.en

Abstract. With an increasing number of shared memory multicore processor architectures, there is a requirement for supporting multiple architectures in automatic parallelizing compilers. The OSCAR (Optimally Scheduled Advanced Multiprocessor) automatic parallelizing compiler is able to parallelize many different sequential programs, such as scientific applications, embedded real-time applications, multimedia applications, and more. OSCAR compiler's features include coarse-grain task parallelization with earliest execution condition analysis, analyzing both data and control dependencies, data locality optimizations over different loop nests with data dependencies, and the ability to generate parallelized code using the OSCAR API 2.1. The OSCAR API 2.1 is compatible with OpenMP for SMP multicores, with additional directives for power control and supporting heterogeneous multicores. This allows for a C or Fortran compiler with OpenMP support to generate parallel machine code for the target multicore. Additionally, using the OSCAR API analyzer allows a sequential-only compiler without OpenMP support to generate machine code for each core separately, which is then linked to one parallel application. Overall, only little configuration changes to the OSCAR compiler are needed to run and optimize OSCAR compiler-generated code on a specific platform. This paper evaluates the performance of OSCAR compiler-generated code on different modern SMP multicore processors, including Intel and AMD x86 processors, an Arm processor, and a RISC-V processor using scientific and multimedia benchmarks in C and Fortran. The results show promising speedups on all platforms, such as a speedup of 7.16 for the swim program of the SPEC2000 benchmarks on an 8-core Intel x86 processor, a speedup of 9.50 for the CG program of the NAS parallel benchmarks on 8 cores of an AMD x86 Processor, a speedup of 3.70 for the BT program of the NAS parallel benchmarks on a 4-core RISC-V processor, and a speedup of 2.64 for the equake program of the SPEC2000 benchmarks on 4 cores of an Arm processor.

© Springer Nature Switzerland AG 2022
X. Li and S. Chandrasekaran (Eds.): LCPC 2021, LNCS 13181, pp. 50–64, 2022.
https://doi.org/10.1007/978-3-030-99372-6_4

Keywords: multicore · parallelizing compiler · OSCAR · multiple platforms · shared memory

1 Introduction

With an increasing number of processor architectures, there is a requirement for supporting multiple architectures in automatic parallelizing compilers.

The OSCAR automatic parallelizing compiler [10] is one such compiler, capable of parallelizing different C and Fortran programs, including scientific applications and simulations, real-time applications, multimedia applications, and more.

Other source-to-source parallelizing compilers have been developed [6,8] to allow for portability of the generated code between different systems and architectures. The OSCAR compiler is additionally able to output code using the OSCAR API 2.1 [15], which is extended from a subset of OpenMP. This allows both OpenMP-capable native compilers to directly compile the OSCAR-compiler generated program, as well as the OSCAR API analyzer to generate separate sequential code for each core of a target system. The resulting sequential code generated by the OSCAR API analyzer for each core then allows a sequential compiler which does not have support for a parallel API such as OpenMP to compile the code for each core and link it to a single parallel program for the target architecture.

Previous evaluations show the performance of OSCAR compiler-generated code on SMP server processors [12], as well as on embedded systems with on-chip shared memory [16].

In this paper, the OSCAR compiler's function, based on multi-grain parallelism and including multiple optimizations such as data localization and cache optimization, will be explained. Additionally, the paper details usage of the OSCAR compiler, targeting systems with and without native compilers supporting OpenMP. Furthermore, this paper analyzes and discusses the performance of programs and benchmarks from the SPEC benchmark suite [9], the NAS parallel benchmark suite [5] and MediaBench II [7], compiled using the OSCAR automatic parallelizing compiler with further optimization techniques such as data localization [22] and cache optimization [13] on different multicore architectures, including an Intel Xeon E5-2650v4 x86 processor, an AMD EPYC 7702P x86 processor, an NVIDIA Carmel ARM®v8.2 processor and a SiFive Freedom U740 RISC-V processor. Neither RISC-V-based processors nor a Zen 2-based processors have been evaluated with the OSCAR compiler before.

2 The OSCAR Automatic Parallelizing Compiler

The OSCAR automatic parallelizing compiler generates parallel code by utilizing multigrain parallelism. Multigrain parallelism includes parallelism of large coarse-grain tasks (coarse-grain parallelism), parallelism of loops (loop-level parallelism) as well as parallelism of individual instructions (statement-level parallelism) [15].

To first exploit coarse grain parallelism, the OSCAR compiler splits the sequential code into macro-tasks. These macro-tasks can be basic blocks of assignments, loops, or function calls. Loops and function calls themselves are then further split into macro-tasks as well. From this, the data and control dependencies between each macro-task can be analyzed, from which, using earliest-execution analysis [10], the macro-tasks are put into a macro-task-graph.

The earliest-execution condition for macro-tasks is twofold:

1. A macro-task must wait for the completion of macro-tasks it is directly data-dependent on.
2. A macro-task must wait until preceding control-dependent macro-tasks have evaluated the conditional branches that guarantee said macro-tasks execution, but the macro-task does not need to wait for the completion of these preceding macro-tasks.

Once these two conditions are met, the macro-task can be scheduled into the macro-task-graph. How these conditions are applied in a real program can be seen in Fig. 1. The first condition, that all macro-tasks that the current macro-task to schedule is data dependent on must have finished, can be seen in the bb19 macro-task. It is scheduled into the macro-task graph once the macro-tasks it is data dependent on, bb2, dosum15, bb17, and bb18, are finished. The second condition can be seen for macro-task bb24. It can already be scheduled after macro-task bb5, since by that time, both its data dependency on bb1 is fulfilled, and, after the conditional branch bb5, it is guaranteed that the control flow will pass bb24.

The tasks in the macro-task graph are occasionally shown to have multiple outgoing or incoming dependency edges.

If these edges pass through a dotted arc (representing a logical or), it means that either of the edges passing through the arc will be followed, caused by a conditional branch in the original program. For outgoing edges, it means that only one of the edges will be followed to execute latter macro-tasks, and for incoming edges, it means that only one edge needs to be satisfied to fulfill the dependency and allow execution of the macro-task.

If the edges pass through a solid arc (representing a logical and), it means that all these edges will be followed, caused mostly by coarse-grain task parallelization. For outgoing edges, it means that all these edges will be followed, executing their respective nodes. For incoming edges, it means that all edges must be satisfied to fulfill the dependency and allow execution of the macro-task.

From the macro-task graph, the individual tasks are assigned to the available processor cores. If runtime fluctuation, for example, due to conditional branches, are expected, the OSCAR compiler utilizes dynamic scheduling at runtime to execute the macro-tasks, otherwise, static scheduling is used. The resulting program uses the one time single level thread generation scheme [19], where the program creates a thread per processor core at program start, and the macro-tasks are then run on these threads respectively.

Loop-level parallelism is then applied to doall-loop and reduction-loop type macro-tasks, if possible. Similarly, statement-level parallelism is applied if it is available in a given macro-task [14].

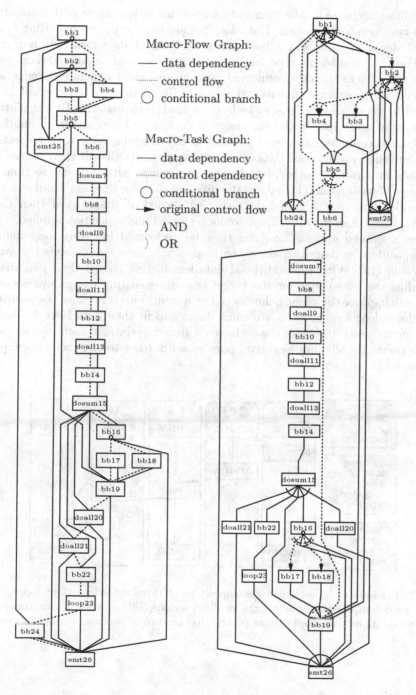

Fig. 1. The macro-flow graph (left) and the macro-task graph (right) of the main training loop of the art benchmark (see Sect. 4)

Additionally, data localization and cache optimization can be performed after macro-task graph generation. Data localization can be performed using loop-aligned decomposition and subsequent generation of data-localization-groups [22]. For this, doall-loop type, reduction-loop type, and sequential-loop type macro-task blocks directly connected only by one data dependence edge are analyzed. In the example macro-task graph in Fig. 1, this would for example be applied to the sequence of macro-tasks from `doall19` to `dosum15`. By calculating which array subscripts in the successive loops are data-dependant on another, the OSCAR compiler can assign sections of the different loops with respective data dependencies into one data-localization-group, which will then be run on one core, in parallel to other data-localization-groups with different sections of the loops of their own. This allows the different data-localization-groups to run in parallel with only minimal data sharing needed at the edge of their data regions. Figure 2 shows an example of loop-aligned decomposition applied.

Further cache optimization can then be performed by using loop-aligned decomposition, as described above, on loops whose data size exceeds the available cache [13]. With the additional data-localization-groups then potentially exceeding the core count for the target system, executing the groups sequentially will improve the cache behavior of the system. This is because the resulting data-dependent loop sections are small enough to fit their data into the cache, reducing the need to replace the cache while iterating through each loop section. Furthermore, by aligning loop-level parallelism borders to the cache lines, performance can be increased.

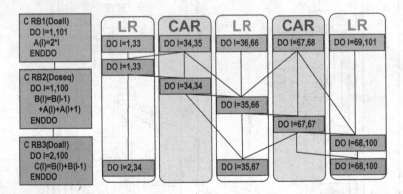

Fig. 2. Example of loop-aligned decomposition of three data-dependent loops. The loops are decomposed into three main localized regions (LR) accessed by one core only, and two commonly accessed regions (CAR) that need to be accessed by multiple cores.

3   Investigated Multicore Architectures

For this paper, four different processor architectures were evaluated. Two x86 processors, one Arm processor, and one RISC-V processor.

The first x86 processor is the Intel Xeon E5-2650v4 12-core processor running at 2.2 GHz with a maximum boost frequency of 2.9 GHz. It has 32 KiB of L1D cache per core, 256 KiB L2 cache per core, and 30 MiB shared L3 cache with a cache line size of 64 [11].

The second x86 processor is the AMD EPYC 7702P 64-core processor running at 2 GHz with a maximum boost frequency of 3.35 GHz. It has 32 KiB of L1D cache per core, 512 KiB L2 cache per core, and 256 MiB shared L3 cache grouped into 4-core clusters with a cache line size of 64 [3]. If a miss in the L3 cache is available in an L2 cache within the same cluster, the L3 cache can load the data from the L2 cache instead of from the main memory [2].

The Arm processor is the NVIDIA Carmel ARM®v8.2 64 Bit 6-core processor running at 1.4 GHz. It is based on ARMv8.2 [4], has 64 KiB L1D cache per core, 2 MiB L2 cache shared between clusters of two cores, and 4 MiB shared L3 cache with a cache line size of 64 [18].

The RISC-V processor is the SiFive Freedom U740 4-core SoC running at 1.2 GHz. It has 32 KiB of L1D cache per application core and 2 MiB shared L2 cache with a cache line size of 64 [21] (Fig. 3).

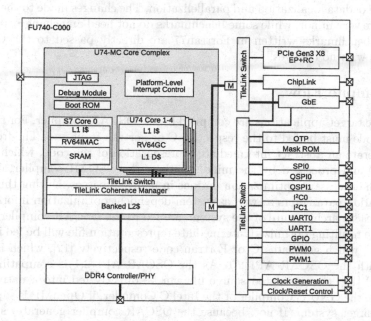

Fig. 3. "FU740-C000 top-level block diagram" by SiFive, Inc. [21]. CC BY-NC-ND 4.0

4   Benchmark Programs

Benchmarks from three different benchmark suites are evaluated in this paper. First, some benchmarks of the NAS parallel benchmark suite [5]. Here, the C version developed by the Real World Computing Project (RWCP), and distributed by the HPCS lab of the University of Tsukuba [20] are used. The specific benchmarks of the NPB suite evaluated are BT, CG, and SP. The SP and BT benchmark both compute the solution of multiple, independent systems of non diagonally dominant equations, an operation used for some computational fluid dynamics algorithms. They differ in the ratio of communication to computation. The CG benchmark applies the conjugate gradient method to a large, sparse, symmetric positive definite matrix to approximate its smallest eigenvalue.

Furthermore, to represent multimedia applications, the MPEG2 encoding benchmark of the MediaBench II suite [7] is evaluated. It is similarly written in C.

Finally, benchmarks of the SPEC2000 floating-point suite [9] are evaluated. From the benchmarks written in C, art and equake are evaluated, and from the benchmarks written in Fortran77, swim is evaluated. The art benchmark test neural network training performance. The equake benchmark simulates seismic wave propagation. The swim benchmark computes a shallow-water model.

The benchmarks in C are manually edited to conform to parallelizable C [17]. Conforming the code to parallelizable C allows the compiler to utilize the full potential of data localization and parallelization. The changes made to the benchmarks are very minor, while some benchmarks do not need any changes at all.

The benchmarks written in Fortran77 are directly passed to the OSCAR compiler with no changes.

5   Compile Flow

First, the target applications are compiled by the OSCAR compiler. For this, the source code must be fed to the respective C or Fortran front-end. The front-end will generate an abstract intermediate representation of the code, which can be analyzed and processed by the middle path of the OSCAR compiler, depending on the necessary optimization options in multiple passes. During this stage, optimization parameters as well as system-dependent optimization information, like the cache architecture of the system, are fed to the OSCAR compiler. Afterward, the resulting optimized intermediate representation file will be fed into the back-end, which generates C or Fortran code respectively [12], which is annotated with the OSCAR API 2.1. As the OSCAR API 2.1 is compatible with OpenMP [15], the generated source file can be directly fed into a native compiler, like the GNU C Compiler or the Intel C Compiler, if OpenMP is supported on the target system. If not, because the OSCAR compiler generates synchronization and data transfer code automatically, the OSCAR API analyzer can be utilized to generate code that contains purely sequential code for each CPU core. This allows a sequential-only compiler to generate machine code for each core separately, that can then be linked to a single, parallel application.

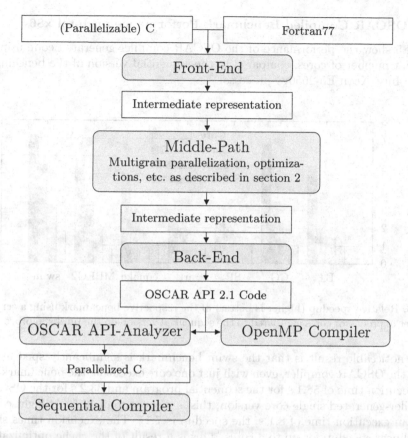

Fig. 4. Compile flow using the OSCAR compiler.

6 Performance of OSCAR Compiler-Parallelized Programs

Unless otherwise noted, all benchmarks, including the sequential reference code and the OSCAR compiler-generated parallelized code, are compiled using the GNU C Compiler with the highest optimization setting (-Ofast) and the correct architecture supplied using -march=. As all architectures investigated in this paper have native compilers with OpenMP support, the OSCAR compiler-generated code was directly compiled without the use of the OSCAR API-Analyzer. In this paper, the parameters of the OSCAR compiler which are adapted for each target architecture are focused on cache parameters such as last-level cache size, cache line size, cache associativity, and the number of cores sharing a last-level cache. Other parameters are kept identical across the different architectures. While micro-optimizations with cost tables for the individual architectures are possible, this paper analyzes the performance when using generic cost tables.

6.1   OSCAR Compiled Benchmark Performance on Intel x86

Figure 5 show the performance of the OSCAR compiler-generated code using a different number of cores, compared to the sequential version of the benchmark on the Intel Xeon E5-2650v4 processor.

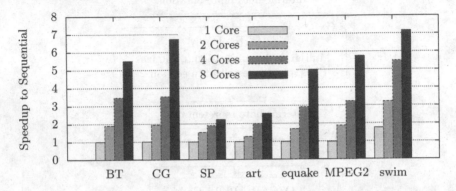

Fig. 5. Relative speedup (higher is better) of the respective benchmark using a certain number of processor cores compared to the sequential version on the Intel x86 processor.

A noticeable result is that the swim benchmark is significantly sped up by using the OSCAR compiler, even with just one core executing the benchmark. At an execution time of 58.1 s for the sequential program and 33.2 s for the OSCAR compiler-generated single-core version, this is a speedup of 1.75. At eight cores, with an execution time of 8.1 s, the speedup is 7.17. The execution times show superlinear speedup for up to 4 cores. This is a result of the cache optimization technique employed by the OSCAR compiler [13] as described in Sect. 2. Table 1 shows the cache statistics of the swim benchmark for the sequential version and the OSCAR compiler-generated versions. These statistics suggest that the OSCAR compiler was able to improve the cache access in the generated code, resulting in the speedup of the benchmark. Furthermore, the MPEG2 encoding benchmark for example, can reduce its execution time from 2.17 s in the sequential version to 0.377 s in the OSCAR compiler-generated eight-core version, for a speedup of 5.75.

To show that the OSCAR compiler can utilize different native compilers, the performances of OSCAR compiler-parallelized benchmarks were tested using the Intel C++ and Fortran Compilers as well. For a better comparison, the sequential reference benchmarks are also compiled using the Intel compilers.

Figure 6 shows both versions' relative speedup to the sequential execution time of the respective benchmark, run on the Intel Xeon E5-2650v4 processor. This shows that the OSCAR compiler can be used in conjunction with the Intel compilers as well to speed up the final result of the execution. The slightly lower relative speedups compared to Fig. 5 are mostly due to the lower sequential execution time of the reference benchmark when compiled with the Intel Compilers at full optimization. For example, while their respective speedups to the

Table 1. Cache statistics of the swim benchmark as measured by `perf`, sequential version compared to OSCAR compiler-generated version.

Program	L1 loads	L1 load misses	L3 loads	L3 load misses
Sequential	$2.3 \cdot 10^{11}$	$1.2 \cdot 10^{11}$	$5.7 \cdot 10^{10}$	$1.1 \cdot 10^{10}$
OSCAR 1 core	$2.3 \cdot 10^{11}$	$6.5 \cdot 10^{10}$	$1.5 \cdot 10^{10}$	$8.2 \cdot 10^{9}$
OSCAR 2 core	$2.2 \cdot 10^{11}$	$6.5 \cdot 10^{10}$	$1.5 \cdot 10^{10}$	$7.1 \cdot 10^{9}$
OSCAR 4 core	$2.2 \cdot 10^{11}$	$6.5 \cdot 10^{10}$	$1.4 \cdot 10^{10}$	$6.1 \cdot 10^{9}$
OSCAR 8 core	$2.2 \cdot 10^{11}$	$6.5 \cdot 10^{10}$	$1.3 \cdot 10^{10}$	$4.1 \cdot 10^{9}$

sequential versions decreased using the Intel compilers, the absolute execution time of the swim benchmark parallelized using the OSCAR compiler targeting eight cores decreased to 5.8 s, while the execution time of the MPEG2 encoding benchmark decreased to 0.234 s.

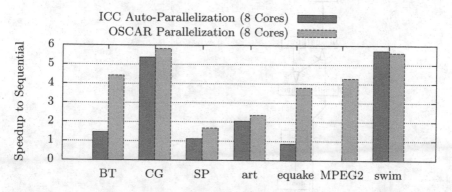

Fig. 6. Relative speedup of the respective benchmark auto-parallelized on 8 cores to its sequential version. Both the sequential version and the OSCAR compiler-generated code used the Intel compiler as the native compiler. The MPEG2 encoding benchmark causes a segmentation fault when compiled with Intel compiler auto-parallelization and run with more than one core, and is thus not shown.

6.2   OSCAR Compiled Benchmark Performance on AMD X86

Figure 7 show the performance of the OSCAR compiler-generated code using a different number of cores, compared to the sequential version of the benchmark on the AMD EPYC7702P processor.

Similar to the Intel processor, the swim benchmark exhibits high single-core performance and some superlinear speedup due to the cache optimization techniques. Additionally, the CG benchmark shows superlinear speedup. As Fig. 8 shows, the main loop of CG features many doall loops and dosum reduction loops in succession with data dependence on another. This macro-task graph structure results in data localization similar to the data localization methods

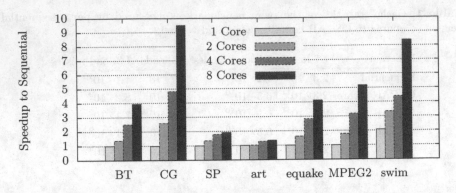

Fig. 7. Relative speedup of the respective benchmark using a certain number of processor cores compared to the sequential version on the AMD x86 processor.

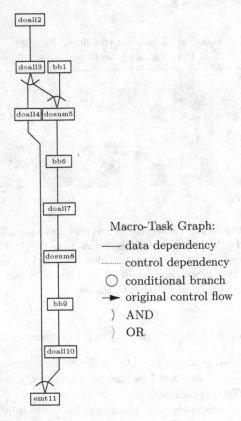

Fig. 8. The macro-task graph of the main loop of the CG benchmark of the NAS parallel benchmark suite (see Sect. 4)

using loop-aligned decomposition [22] described in Sect. 2. The data localization is able to improve the performance of the benchmark with multiple cores and causes the superlinear speedup, decreasing overall execution time from 0.86 s in the sequential version to 0.09 s using the OSCAR compiler-generated eight-core version for a 9.5 speedup.

The OSCAR compiler uses operation cost tables for estimating task length for scheduling. These benchmarks used generic tables for all benchmarks. Customizing this table for the AMD EPYC 7702P processor would allow for an improvement of the speedup of the art benchmark on this system. For the art benchmark without customizing the operation cost table, the execution time was only reduced from 4.76 s in the sequential version to 3.52 s using the OSCAR compiler-generated eight-core version for a speedup of 1.35.

6.3 OSCAR Compiled Benchmark Performance on Arm

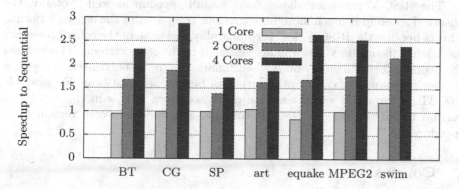

Fig. 9. Relative speedup of the respective benchmark using a certain number of processor cores compared to the sequential version on the Arm processor.

Figure 9 shows the performance of the OSCAR compiler-generated code using a different number of cores, compared to the sequential version of the benchmark on the NVIDIA Carmel ARM®v8.2 64 Bit processor.

The Arm processor shows overall good speedup for the different benchmarks. While the cache optimization applied to the swim benchmark is noticeable, it is much smaller compared to the effects on the Intel and AMD CPU's. Overall, good speedup is observed, with for example the equake benchmark's execution time decreasing from 19.0 s in the sequential version to 7.18 s using the OSCAR compiler-generated four-core version for a speedup of 2.64.

6.4 OSCAR Compiled Benchmark Performance on RISC-V

Figure 10 show the performance of the OSCAR compiler-generated code using a different number of cores, compared to the sequential version of the benchmark on the SiFive Freedom U740 processor.

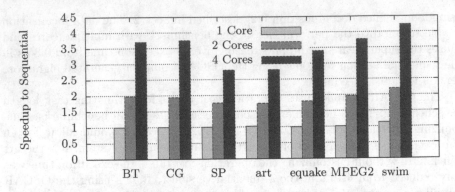

Fig. 10. Relative speedup of the respective benchmark using a certain number of processor cores compared to the sequential version on the RISC-V processor.

The RISC-V processor shows good overall speedup as well. Notably, the observed speedup is much more homogeneous compared to the other platforms. This is because the RISC-V SoC is comparably slower than the other processors used, while the memory performance is similar to the other systems. This reduces the overall effect of memory on the benchmarks, both the bottlenecks, as well as the positive impact of cache optimization for benchmarks like swim. For example the BT benchmark's execution time decreased from 2041 s in the sequential version to 551 s using the OSCAR compiler-generated four-core version for a speedup of 3.7.

7   Conclusion

This paper shows how the OSCAR automatic parallelizing compiler can utilize multigrain parallelism to generate parallelized code from different programs and benchmarks for various architectures from embedded multicores to high-performance processors. This code can then be compiled for the respective architectures using a native compiler of the system, like the Intel C and Fortran Compilers or the GNU C and Fortran Compilers. By utilizing the OSCAR API 2.1 and the OSCAR API analyzer, it is even possible to generate sequential code for each core of a system, which allows OSCAR compiler-generated code to be run on systems whose native compilers do not support a parallel API such as OpenMP. Overall, this paper finds that the OSCAR compiler is able to automatically parallelize a variety of benchmarks, including scientific simulations, media applications, and machine learning applications, written in C and Fortran with good speedup. Measuring the benchmark programs showed good performances, such as a speedup of 7.16 for the swim program of the SPEC2000 benchmarks, a speedup of 6.73 for the CG program of the NAS parallel benchmarks, and a speedup of 5.75 for the MPEG2 encoding benchmark on 8 cores of an Intel x86 processor. Similarly, on 8 cores of the AMD x86 processor, speedups such as 9.50 for the CG program of the NAS parallel benchmarks, a speedup of 8.39 for the swim program of the SPEC2000 benchmarks, and a speedup of 3.94 on the BT benchmark of the NAS parallel were observed. On the 4-core SiFive RISC-V processor, speedups including a speedup of 3.70 for the BT program of the NAS parallel benchmarks on a 4-core, a speedup of 2.80 for the SP program of the NAS parallel benchmarks, and a speedup of 3.40 for the equake program of the SPEC2000 benchmarks. Finally, on 4 cores of an NVIDIA Arm processor, observed speedups include 2.64 for the equake program of the SPEC2000 benchmarks, 2.87 for the CG program of the NAS parallel benchmarks, and 1.86 for the art program of the SPEC2000 benchmarks.

These speedups are similar to the previous performance of OSCAR generated code on the RP2 processor platform [1]. This shows that the OSCAR compiler can achieve good speedup and performance for benchmarks on different architectures with different instruction sets as well. The OSCAR compiler proves to be able to handle parallelizing code for a variety of current architectures, including embedded systems and high-performance processors, without extensive per-system tuning, using default parameters and cost tables.

Due to advanced optimization techniques such as cache optimization and data localization, superlinear speedup can be achieved for some benchmarks.

References

1. Adhi, B.A., Kashimata, T., Takahashi, K., Kimura, K., Kasahara, H.: Compiler software coherent control for embedded high performance multicore. IEICE Trans. Electron. **E103.C**(3), 85–97 (2020). https://doi.org/10.1587/transele. 2019LHP0008
2. Advanced Micro Devices Inc.: Software Optimization Guide for AMD Family 17h Processors (2017)
3. Advanced Micro Devices Inc.: Preliminary Processor Programming Reference (PPR) for AMD Family 17h Model 31h, Revision B0 Processors (2020)
4. Arm Limited: Arm® Architecture Reference Manual, Armv8, for Armv8-A architecture profile (2021)
5. Bailey, D.H., et al.: The NAS parallel benchmarks summary and preliminary results. In: Supercomputing 1991: Proceedings of the 1991 ACM/IEEE Conference on Supercomputing, pp. 158–165 (1991). https://doi.org/10.1145/125826.125925
6. Blume, W., Doallo, R., Eigenmann, R., Grout, J., Hoeflinger, J., Lawrence, T.: Parallel programming with Polaris. Computer **29**(12), 78–82 (1996). https://doi. org/10.1109/2.546612
7. Fritts, J.E., Steiling, F.W., Tucek, J.A., Wolf, W.: MediaBench II video: expediting the next generation of video systems research. Microprocess. Microsyst. **33**(4), 301–318 (2009). https://doi.org/10.1016/j.micpro.2009.02.010
8. Hall, M., et al.: Maximizing multiprocessor performance with the SUIF compiler. Computer **29**(12), 84–89 (1996). https://doi.org/10.1109/2.546613
9. Henning, J.L.: SPEC CPU2000: measuring CPU performance in the new millennium. Computer **33**(7), 28–35 (2000). https://doi.org/10.1109/2.869367
10. Honda, H., Kasahara, H.: Coarse grain parallelism detection scheme of a Fortran program. Syst. Comput. Jpn. **22**(12), 24–36 (1991). https://doi.org/10.1002/scj. 4690221203

11. Intel Corp.: Intel® 64 and IA-32 Architectures Software Developer's Manual (2021)
12. Ishizaka, K., Miyamoto, T., Shirako, J., Obata, M., Kimura, K., Kasahara, H.: Performance of OSCAR multigrain parallelizing compiler on SMP servers. In: Eigenmann, R., Li, Z., Midkiff, S.P. (eds.) LCPC 2004. LNCS, vol. 3602, pp. 319–331. Springer, Heidelberg (2005). https://doi.org/10.1007/11532378_23
13. Ishizaka, K., Obata, M., Kasahara, H.: Coarse grain task parallel processing with cache optimization on shared memory multiprocessor. In: Dietz, H.G. (ed.) LCPC 2001. LNCS, vol. 2624, pp. 352–365. Springer, Heidelberg (2003). https://doi.org/10.1007/3-540-35767-X_23
14. Kimura, K., et al.: Multigrain parallel processing on compiler cooperative chip multiprocessor. In: 9th Annual Workshop on Interaction between Compilers and Computer Architectures (INTERACT 2005), pp. 11–20 (2005). https://doi.org/10.1109/INTERACT.2005.9
15. Kimura, K., et al.: OSCAR API v2.1: extensions for an advanced accelerator control scheme to a low-power multicore API. In: 17th Workshop on Compilers for Parallel Computing (2013)
16. Kimura, K., Mase, M., Mikami, H., Miyamoto, T., Shirako, J., Kasahara, H.: OSCAR API for real-time low-power multicores and its performance on multicores and SMP servers. In: Gao, G.R., Pollock, L.L., Cavazos, J., Li, X. (eds.) LCPC 2009. LNCS, vol. 5898, pp. 188–202. Springer, Heidelberg (2010). https://doi.org/10.1007/978-3-642-13374-9_13
17. Mase, M., Onozaki, Y., Kimura, K., Kasahara, H.: Parallelizable c and its performance on low power high performance multicore processors (2010)
18. NVIDIA Corp.: NVIDIA Jetson Xavier NX System-on-Module Data Sheet (2020)
19. Obata, M., Shirako, J., Kaminaga, H., Ishizaka, K., Kasahara, H.: Hierarchical parallelism control for multigrain parallel processing. In: Pugh, B., Tseng, C.-W. (eds.) LCPC 2002. LNCS, vol. 2481, pp. 31–44. Springer, Heidelberg (2005). https://doi.org/10.1007/11596110_3
20. Real world computing project: Omni OpenMP Compiler Project. http://www.hpcs.cs.tsukuba.ac.jp/omni-compiler/. Accessed 18 July 2021
21. SiFive Inc.: SiFive FU740-C000 Manual (2021)
22. Yoshida, A., Koshizuka, K., Kasahara, H.: Data-localization for Fortran macro-dataflow computation using partial static task assignment. In: Proceedings of the 10th International Conference on Supercomputing, ICS 1996, pp. 61–68. Association for Computing Machinery, New York (1996). https://doi.org/10.1145/237578.237586

Accelerators

LC-MEMENTO: A Memory Model for Accelerated Architectures

Kiran Ranganath[1]($\boxtimes$), Jesun Firoz[2], Joshua Suetterlein[2]($\boxtimes$), Joseph Manzano[2], Andres Marquez[2], Mark Raugas[2], and Daniel Wong[1]

[1] University of California Riverside, Riverside, CA 92521, USA
{krang006,danwong}@ucr.edu
[2] Pacific Northwest National Laboratory, Richland, WA 99352, USA
{jesun.firoz,joshua.suetterlein,joseph.manzano,andres.marquez,
mark.raugas}@pnnl.gov

Abstract. With the advent of heterogeneous architectures, in particular, with the ubiquity of multi-GPU systems, it is becoming increasingly important to manage device memory efficiently in order to reap the benefits of the additional core count. To date, such responsibility mainly falls on the programmer where device-to-host data communication (and vice versa), if not done properly, may incur costly memory transfer operations and synchronization. The problem may be compounded by additional requirement to maintain system-wide memory consistency that may involve expensive synchronization overhead. In this paper, we present **L**ocation **C**onsistency **M**emory **M**odel for **En**hanced **T**ransfer **O**perations (LC-MEMENTO). This framework considers incorporating runtime techniques for multi-GPU memory management to support relaxed synchronization semantics and memory transfer operations automatically. Specifically, we implement a relaxed form of a memory consistency model based on the Location Consistency (LC) in an Asynchronous Many-Task Runtime (ARTS) and demonstrate that, this memory model enables additional optimization opportunities for the three representative applications encompassing different computational patterns (scientific computation, graphs, data streaming, etc.).

1 Introduction

In recent years, the widespread adoption and integration of accelerators as part of the High-Performance Computing (HPC) ecosystems have presented several unique challenges to the runtimes and software stacks with regards to effectively managing massive heterogeneous computational resources and interacting with the hierarchical memory subsystems. Among these accelerators, General Purpose Graphic Processing Units (GPGPUs) are the most prevalent ones that are either currently in use or in the roadmaps of the current and future generation of the most powerful supercomputers [29]. This trend has sparked a new wave of research in software stacks and runtime libraries to fully utilize the current heterogeneity of these designs, e.g., [27]. Some of the most important challenges in this area include the coordination among computational and memory

© Springer Nature Switzerland AG 2022
X. Li and S. Chandrasekaran (Eds.): LCPC 2021, LNCS 13181, pp. 67–82, 2022.
https://doi.org/10.1007/978-3-030-99372-6_5

resources, efficient communication between parallel components, and productive use of additional resources e.g., high performance networks.

Traditionally, the burden of managing all these challenges have fallen on the application programmer or the user due to the lack of proper runtime support. Hence, manually managing these resources have made the development of novel, high-performance implementations of interesting applications a very onerous process. However, one of the most promising programming execution paradigms to effectively support programmers to exploit massive parallelism available on recent accelerator-based systems are the Asynchronous Many-Task (AMT) runtimes. These frameworks are designed to utilize the underlying computational substrates by dividing the computation into well-defined tasks which can be executed asynchronously. Nonetheless, support for effective runtime scheduling for memory management and fine-grained synchronization can be improved.

To support more flexible frameworks that can more effectively map resources without programmer intervention, we consider a previously proposed memory consistency model, Location Consistency [10], and re-purpose this consistency model for multi-GPU systems. Thus, this paper introduces LC-MEMENTO: a new runtime extension to an AMT runtime named ARTS [25] to support accelerated architectures. These extensions include a runtime-managed transparent scheduler for multi-GPUs systems designed to exploit new multi-GPU designs; and a novel memory model extension, designed to increase the productivity of programmers and the performance of current data analytics workflows. The contributions of this paper are as follows: (1) A novel GPU cache-based memory model based on the Location Consistency Model [10] with extensions for polymorphic[1] (relaxed) synchronization/collective operations; (2) a scheduler framework that automatically exploits multi-accelerator environments for task scheduling and memory management without user intervention; and (3) a performance analysis of three important data analytics kernels (STREAM and Random Access benchmark from HPC Challenge benchmark suite [17], as well as the well-known Breadth-first Search (BFS) from graph analytics) that demonstrate the advantages of our framework. In addition, we also compare our approach with current technologies such as Unified Virtual Memory (UVM).

This paper is organized as follows. Section 2 explains the necessary concepts that permeates this paper such memory consistency and the basics of ARTS. Section 3 introduces and explains the LC-MEMENTO implementation under ARTS. Section 4 demonstrate the effectiveness of our techniques via experimental results, obtained on a Summit supercomputer Node and on a DGX-1 Volta GPU based nodes. In Sect. 5, we showcase select state-of-the-art research that might complement or enhance our line of research. Finally, Sect. 6 discusses our conclusions and future directions.

2   Background

To fully explain the design and impact of LC-MEMENTO, this section briefly discusses the concepts behind memory models and location consistency, as well

---

[1] Their ancillary functionality can be set and reset across different program's phases.

as introduces the overall design of the Abstract Runtime System (ARTS), a runtime in which the concepts of LC-MEMENTO are implemented.

2.1 Memory Consistency Models

As computer architectures are progressively becoming more complex, the exposition of the hierarchical and hybrid memory subsystem requires giving consideration to unique challenges. The introduction of reorder buffers, bypass memory queues, and the availability of multi-core and many-core processors with different cache levels introduced many new complex issues related to the ordering and the visibility of memory operations in these systems. The challenges associated with the questions of when operations on memory locations can be reordered or when two distinct parallel actors will observe an updated value on a fixed memory address, became the crux of many optimization-related research in architecture and system software (e.g., [16]). The rules of the ordering and visibility of these memory operations is roughly collected under a **memory consistency model** [3]. Under this paradigm, the strength of a model is inversely dictated by the allowed cardinality of the set of possible orderings. In other words, the more possible chains of valid memory operators that a model allows, the weaker it is. Weaker models can allow for the same variable to have different values across executions if not correctly synchronized. The most common and one of the strongest models is called **sequential consistency**. Under this model, the ordering of the memory operations and their visibility are *as if* it follows the program order across all parallel actors in the system. This may imply a highly synchronized underlying network (like a bus) for which this type of coordination is possible. Such stringent model may prevent certain re-ordering operations that may be beneficial from the perspective of the hardware. For example, a store and a load can be reordered if they do not pose any dependency or the values of one store that overwrites the other may not need to be updated outside the local memory buffer or cache line. For this purpose, several weaker models have been proposed such as CDAG [13] for distributed systems and lazy release consistency [18]. Memory models are also very useful to understand the memory behavior in parallel computation. A notable one is *Location Consistency (LC)*.

Location Consistency. Location Consistency [10] is, arguably, the weakest "practical"[2] memory model. This model weakens the visibility requirements of the classical execution models by allowing a single variable to have multiple values at the same time in different parts of the system, typically by residing in a local piece of memory (cache for example), unless collapsed **explicitly** by the user. The aggregated values of a memory location is called its Partial Ordered Set or POMSET. The model has three operations: a program read, a program write and the synchronized acquire and release pair. For normal program reads and writes,

---

[2] A practical memory model is one that can be used by application developers to write non-chaotic codes since all of its non-determinism can be contained by special operators.

the location will keep the written values and return a value from it when a read is requested. The ordering of these operations is not respected when no acquire and release pairs are presented. In addition, two consecutive reads might return different values from the POMSET in the same execution. For example, if T_0 follows the instruction sequence: $R_1 = X; X = 1$ and T_1 executes the following instruction stream: $R_2 = X; X = 2$, the result $R_1 = 2$ and $R_2 = 1$ is not allowed under other memory models (both sequential and coherence memory models would disallowed this result), but it is considered a legal case under LC since the writes can be reordered (see [15] for a further discussion about the original LC properties and proofs). The semantics of the acquire/release pairs operations follow the classical view of entry consistency [5]. In this model, the acquire and release pair establishes a region of code for which its constituting instructions must be contained inside their boundaries in terms of execution and completion. However, instructions originating before and after the pair can be reordered, started or completed at any point of the execution (even inside the acquire/release pair code block). LC enhances this concept by ensuring that the POMSET is collapsed to a single value after the release operation so that any consequent reads will return that value and only that value. The enhanced semantics of the acquire and release pairs plus the relaxed constrains for the other memory operations allow reordering optimizations to take place in both the software stack and in the hardware. Such freedom in reordering allows fine-grained asynchronous frameworks to take advantage of latency hiding techniques as long as the application can support some degree of error such as in certain data and graph workflows.

2.2 The Abstract Runtime System: ARTS

ARTS is designed as a best of breed runtime from our previous experience with OCR [9], GMT [7], and AM++ [30] leveraging key features from each runtime. ARTS supports parallelism via asynchronous tasking, active messages, and lightweight multithreading. To enable synchronization, ARTS provides a global address space which can be used to access segments of memory called data blocks. In order to support data analytic workloads, ARTS provides methods for termination detection (i.e. quiescence), asynchronous memory operations (e.g. get/put), and remote atomics. As a dataflow inspired runtime, applications are expressed as a Directed Acyclic Graph (DAG) of fine-grain tasks, with each vertex representing a task and an edge between two vertices depicting dependencies between these two tasks. The DAG is constructed dynamically; it is both created and evaluated at runtime. Data is passed between tasks via typed segmented memory chunks a.k.a data blocks. Besides basic typing information, the data blocks under ARTS have no inherent semantic meaning and follow an enhanced version of Entry Consistency plus DAG consistency called CDAG. Under this model, acquire and release pairs are defined at the beginning and end of the computational tasks and the system ordering is imposed by the DAG structure of the computational graph with the extra caveat that possible concurrent writes must be ordered by the DAG explicitly. Dependencies between tasks are expressed using a signaling API. This API is the vehicle for the movement of data blocks around the underlying cluster. Both tasks and data blocks are identified with a globally unique ID (GUID) facilitating access throughout the cluster via the runtime. To evaluate the DAG, the runtime employs five layers, our tasking/scheduling layer, an out-of-order engine that allows reservations of resources dynamically even when dependencies are not ready, the global address space/memory model presented above, several network layers, and an introspection framework. Each layer is informed by the ARTS abstract machine model which is used to describe the underlying computational substrate. While the ARTS execution model was originally developed for traditional CPU architectures, the following sections discuss its extension to a multi-GPU substrate.

2.3 NVIDIA CUDA Programming and Execution Environment

CUDA has rapidly become the de-facto language of GPGPU accelerators which speaks to the fact that NVIDIA GPUs are the dominant force behind the accelerator based supercomputers (for the current generation). This notoriety has amassed a vast of collection of highly optimized libraries for different domains, from scientific, data processing, and machine learning. Moreover, the multi-GPU environment has become a staple on the high performance field. Such situations presents challenges as how to effectively use all available computational resources and how to coordinate data movement across them (challenges familiar to distributed computing). The current available solutions include the concepts of kernel streams [24] that allow the scheduling of individual kernels to separate GPUs concurrently as well as ordering them in case of dependencies (i.e. kernels within a stream are executed in order). In the case of memory, current NVIDIA hardware provide the concept of Unified Memory (UVM) which allows several GPUs and the host to share a memory space which is controlled at a page level. These solutions, although very helpful, have severe shortcomings. The stream based approach would leave the entire scheduling and managing process to the application users creating a very onerous and error-prone development process. The UVM-based approach has the disadvantage that accesses and reuse happen at page boundaries which might be too big for certain applications. Taking all these concepts together, the reordering capabilities of weak memory models, the flexibility of asynchronous runtime systems and the building blocks provided by the current state of the art accelerators, we can build a framework to explore enhanced scheduler, and memory model extensions that will benefit accelerators running on the most powerful computers available.

3 LC-MEMENTO Design and Implementation

To create a productive and performance oriented programming framework for multi accelerator environments, we enhance the existing memory model with new semantics to combine synchronization and computation in a single operation (polymorphic collective/synchronization ops) such that the cost of synchronization can be amortized with these collective like operators. This memory model is implemented through the use of an accelerator cache which at the same time can exploit locality when available. Moreover, this is built upon a scheduler framework that distributes the work across multiple GPUs while providing policies to manage work and storage if the user requires. Each enhancement is explained below.

3.1 Asynchronous Runtime Scheduler for Accelerators

To indicate which tasks should execute on a GPU, we provide a specialized LC-MEMENTO task. This task also allows the user to enumerate the required data blocks via their GUIDs. The Data block GUIDs can be provided both at task creation or during the runtime prior to task execution. These GPU tasks are not scheduled until all task dependencies are met, and are not executed on a device until the required data blocks are present in the GPU's data block cache. In addition to user written GPU functions, we leverage the vast library of optimized domain specific libraries by providing concurrency abstractions to execute existing libraries easing LC-MEMENTO/ARTS GPU development.

When a GPU task's dependencies have been met, the task is scheduled based on user configurable predefined load-balancing schemes designed to explore the trade-off between parallelism and memory consumption. To run parallel kernels and to facilitate data movement between the host and GPUs, we leverage the parallel NVIDIA stream constructs. Prior to running a kernel, the appropriate data blocks are moved to the selected GPU (assuming that the data block is not already present) by the runtime. Further, the runtime maintains a directory of data block GUIDs on the host to manage the memory of a given GPU's cache. By tracking this information at the runtime level on the host, we are able to schedule work according to heuristics to promote parallelism, locality, or memory efficiency. Once a kernel is completed, the appropriate tasks are signaled and dirty (modified) data blocks are moved back to the host. Copies of valid data blocks remain on the device, until a garbage collection process is executed by an idle host thread in order to promote temporal locality.

There are several benefits of the runtime maintaining both memory and scheduling. First, work can be load balanced across GPUs transparent to the user since the correctness is being guaranteed by the application DAG. The second benefit comes from the runtime managing memory. By specifying the data block requirements, the user can ensure there is sufficient memory to run a given kernel prior to execution working to eliminate out-of-memory errors during runtime. In addition, the runtime ensures the transfer of appropriate data block to the device prior to the execution of the kernels. The final benefit is the virtualization of memory at a sub-page level which can have significant impact on irregular applications.

3.2 Memory Models for Accelerators

One of the key limitations to location consistency is the mechanism used to reduce the POMSET. Particularly, how a user can indicate which value the

POMSET should be reduced to. For some applications, the most recently written or random value is acceptable. While this is reasonable from a hardware implementation perspective, we find this less useful to the application programmer. Instead we propose performing reduction operations on the POMSET. Appropriate operations should be associative and preferably idempotent.[3] Since we are implementing our solution in software, operations are not required to be atomic. Examples of these operations include addition, subtraction, multiplication, min, max, AND, OR, and XOR.

Rather than implementing LC for each level of access granularity (memory location, cache line, data structure, etc.), we maintain consistency at the ARTS's memory abstraction: the data block. Under LC-MEMENTO, data blocks are placed inside a software cache on each accelerator, with the CPU maintaining a global directory of their GUIDs similar to a directory based distributed memory cache [14]. Besides each data block being typed as either read or write, we extend the data block with an LC-MEMENTO based type which we denote as LC data block or LCDAB. On a cache miss when accessing a LCDAB, the host transfers a copy to the accelerator. In response, the accelerator is free to access the LCDAB without any synchronization with other accelerators or other CPU's data block (LCDAB or otherwise) copies. When a LCDAB is evicted, the host pulls the accelerator's copy and perform a merge operation (which can be user-defined) between the host and devices copies. If the user requires a consistent state across all devices, they can use a synchronization API call to ensure that the global view of the data is consistent. This operation usually translates to merge operations to be performed on all of the data block copies across the system using both the ARTS CDAG protocol for internode consistency and LC-MEMENTO for intranode one. Currently, LC-MEMENTO has two different merge techniques. The first one is a reduction which copies the LCDABs from each accelerators to the host and performs the merge on the host. While this implementation provides semantically correct results, it is less efficient as the reduction is performed serially on the host. The second reduction mode implements a dynamic reduction tree across accelerators using their optimized collective operator libraries. As the tree is created, we identify which accelerators have a valid copy of the LCDAB. Next, we form a reduction tree based on the host/accelerator topology, ensuring that a high bandwidth is maintained across all participating accelerators. The data block is then sent to its peer accelerator, where it performs the merge operation in a kernel based on the size of the LCDAB (e.g., leveraging SIMT parallelism for NVIDIA GPUs). Once all the accelerator connected through the links have reduced their data, the results are transferred and merged with the host's copy.

In some cases, the operations used to perform are not idempotent (i.e. add, XOR, etc.). In these cases, we provide an API to initialize zero copy LCDABs on the accelerators. We have found this sufficient for implementing benchmarks such as HPC Challenge's Random Access.

---

[3] A concept in computer science and mathematics in which operators can be applied multiple times without changing the results/state of the computation after the first application.

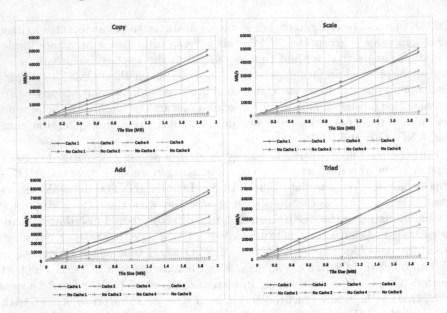

Fig. 1. STREAM benchmark results, demonstrating the usefulness of caching and larger tile size.

4 Evaluation

We evaluate our proposed framework using three of the cornerstone kernels in data and graph analytics. We conduct our experiments on a DGX-1 Volta-based platform. We compile our code with CUDA 9 and GCC 8 to evaluate our framework. The DGX-1 system has 8 Volta GPUs connected to a x86 host with 16 CPU cores. The DGX-1 GPUs are connected in two grids of four and then connected across by their closest GPUs.

4.1 STREAM Benchmark

The STREAM benchmark is a part of the HPC Challenge benchmark suite [17]. It is designed to test the sustainable bandwidth of a memory subsystem focusing on the performance of its cache. The benchmark consists of four kernels, copy, scale, add, and triad. Each kernel operates on two to three operands in a loop with a stride of one. The kernels themselves show little reuse within a kernel, but data can be cached across kernel invocations. The operation intensity for copy/scale and add/triad is 16 bytes to 1 op and 24 bytes to two ops respectively. For LC-MEMENTO, we tile the input arrays so they can be distributed by our scheduler. This benchmark is written for a single node, and we tested it on the DGX-1 system with a problem size of 15 MBs. Figure 1 presents our results across multiple GPUs as we scale the tile size. In the subsequent figures, "X" in the legend "Cache X" or "UMA X" denotes the number of GPU(s) used.

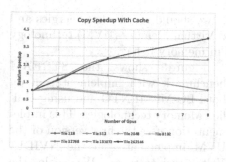 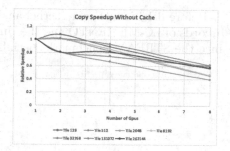

Fig. 2. Copy with and without cache

By tiling the data into manageable data blocks (to avoid out-of-memory error), by transferring the tiled data transparently to the device with the help of the runtime scheduler as the kernels become ready to execute, and by enabling reuse of data across different kernels to take advantage of spatial locality, LC-MEMENTO can achieve better bandwidth utilization, compared to the case with no available caching (Figure 1). Another insight is that small tile sizes do not scale well since the cost of launching multiple kernels (tasks) cannot be efficiently amortized. Thus, the best performance is achieved with the largest tile sizes. Finally, it is worthwhile to point out the difference in operational intensity and performance between the different kernels. In these cases, both add and triad outperform copy and scale in their performance.

Figures 2 and 3 present the relative speedup of the copy and add benchmarks. In the case of larger tile sizes, we can achieve a peak speed up of 4× running on 8 GPUs. This is because at this size, we achieve a higher bandwidth when moving data onto the GPU.

In Fig. 4, we scale the tile size proportionally with the problem size to find the maximum speedup achievable on a single node using 8 GPUs. We see that the performance levels stabilize around 5×, as we saturate the bandwidth available to the GPUs. These benchmarks illustrate the importance of data movement. To scale, we require tasks to either have high reuse, or are large enough to saturate the bandwidth to the GPUs. If the reuse is low, we will always be bound by data movement.

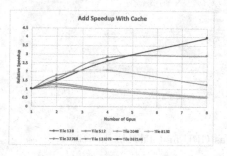 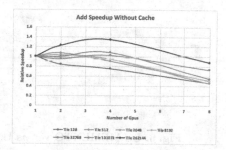

Fig. 3. Add with and without cache

Before delving into more kernel analysis, we should revisit the synergies and discords of LC-MEMENTO and the Unified Virtual Memory (UVM) technology since the STREAM benchmark specializes in memory behavior.

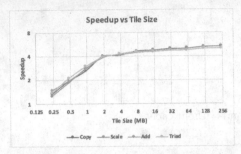

Fig. 4. Speedup while varying tile size

Figure 5 shows the STREAM benchmark with implementation on both LC-MEMENTO and using Unified Memory technologies. This implementation uses the first version of the UVM implemented in the NVIDIA Volta architectures. We scale the problem size and tile size proportionally in each of the eight GPUs. This figure shows that the maximum speedup achievable in these experiments is related to the max bandwidth and kernel invocation rate. This translates to around of 4× improvement over UMA at the largest tile size.

Figure 6 showcase that the copy and add kernels as we increase the tile size with more GPUs. Although both frameworks decreases as bigger tile sizes and more GPUs are introduces, we observe that LC-MEMENTO scales up to the size of one MB tile while UVM does not scale in any situation. This seems to be a side effect of congestion and saturation of bandwidth as we increase the GPUs. UVM can overcome LC-

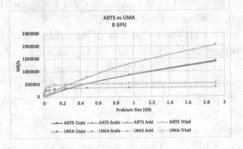

Fig. 5. STREAM ARTS vs UVM

MEMENTO in the largest cases when using only one GPU due to its hardware support. However, LC-MEMENTO helps with concurrency in the other cases.

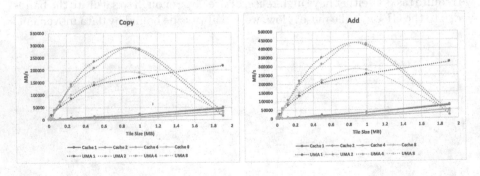

Fig. 6. LC-MEMENTO versus UVM as GPU and Tile size increases.

4.2   Random Access Benchmark

The Random Access benchmark is also part of the HPC Challenge benchmark suite [17]. This benchmark generates random updates to a large table that is designed to stress the memory subsystem. The benchmark metric is defined as Giga Updates per Seconds (GUPS). During each table access, a bit-wise XOR operation is performed to value with a random number. Afterwards, the table can be check for consistency in case that weak synchronization is used. We implement this benchmark to first generate the 1024 updates per SIMT thread in the system. Next, we pass this update frontier to a task with a tile of the table and perform all the updates that correspond to that tile. At the end, we synchronize the results using the LC extensions. The benchmark states that a process should only look ahead by 1024 updates (designed with MPI ranks in mind). We have relaxed this constraint to 1024 per thread since this better utilizes the GPU while still maintaining the benchmark's objective. We run this benchmark on a single node of the DGX-1 system using 16 host threads and scaling the number of GPUs from one to eight. We use a table size of 1.25 GB and divide our tiles evenly across the GPUs. We perform 2684354560 updates. As a baseline we provide a Unified Memory version for comparison.

From Fig. 7, we observe that LC-MEMENTO's performance achieve a relative speedup of 2.8. While we are not suffering the effects of synchronization, we still observe the network bottleneck of data movement and kernel invocation. Without work to amortize this cost, scaling the kernel's performance is difficult. The Unified Memory baseline exhibits good scalability for one to five GPUs. We believe that at six GPUs the cost of on-demand paging (at a size of 4K) becomes too onerous and grinds its performance to a halt. In the case of using above six GPUs, LC-MEMENTO maintains its performance while UVM is overwhelmed.

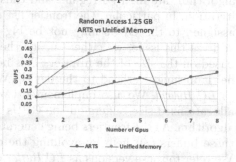

Fig. 7. Random Access benchmark on ARTS vs using Unified Virtual Memory.

4.3   Breadth-First Search

Breadth-first search is one of the most important and common graph kernels that is widely used to evaluate the performance of HPC systems for irregular workloads. We implemented the k-level asynchronous Breadth-first search algorithm presented in [8]. In this algorithm, the level of asynchronous is controlled with the k parameter (i.e., when k is equal to one, the algorithm is fully synchronous; otherwise, the algorithm is fully asynchronous for k steps with redundant work for straggler computation) which is taken advantage by the LC-MEMENTO framework. This is thanks to LC-MEMENTO's flexibility with global reduction

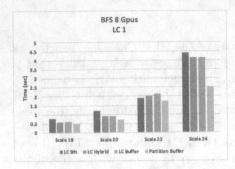
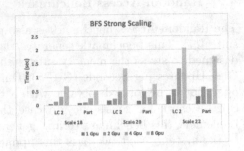

Fig. 8. Experimental results with the BFS kernel. On the left, we report the execution time of different variants of the BFS kernel on 8 GPUs. On the right, we report strong scaling results. Here, Scale X denotes a graph input with 2^X vertices, generated with the RMAT synthetic graph generator from the Graph500 benchmark.

operations and their semantics. This basic variant based on the extended location consistency is denoted as *LC BFS* in Fig. 8. However, notice that, graph algorithms are highly irregular and thus can generate uneven workload in each iteration. In particular, the frontier list (i.e. the next set of vertices to explore) assigned to the GPUs may not be big enough to require GPU execution. To address this issue, we either engage the CPU or a GPU to explore a frontier, based on the size of the frontier. This helps to avoid the data transfer and kernel launching overhead to the device. We denote this version of our algorithm as *LC Hybrid*. We also implemented two additional versions of BFS, where we allocate fixed-size buffers on the GPUs as a buffer pool, before the start of the algorithm. As the frontiers being generated can be of variable size, pre-allocating these buffers can help by avoiding the cost of re-allocation, in every iteration. We refer to these versions as *LC Buffer* and *Partition Buffer (partitioned buffer without LC)*. Setting the value of k to 1 will also result in a level-synchronous or label-setting BFS algorithm, similar to Graph500 [28] benchmark, redundant work is held back and vertices are assigned at the final level.

We evaluate the performance of these algorithms running on a single node of the DGX-1 system using 16 host CPU threads and eight GPUs ad report the results in Fig. 8. The input graphs are generated with Graph500's RMAT generator. Each vertex has a uniform degree of 16 edges. We generated graphs of scale 18, 20, 22, and 24. Here, scale X denotes a graph with 2^X vertices. We observe that "partition buffer" variant of the algorithm performs best, while the LC buffered and hybrid versions demonstrate similar performance. This is not surprising, since the input graphs have uniform degree distribution, hence the load is well-balanced and have little chance to benefiting from the extended LC memory model. However, we anticipate that, graphs with power-law degree distribution, in which a few high-degree vertices exist, will benefit from the extended LC memory model. Our strong scaling plot (Fig. 8) shows that scalability suffers due to the overhead of small search frontiers per tile and no re-use.

We also vary the frequency of synchronization when applying LC-MEMENTO and report the results in Fig. 9. As with many graph applications, we observe that the result tends to be data-dependent (size of the frontier being generated) and not particularly related to the size of the graphs. For example, for graphs with scales of 18 and 24, we see that synchronizing in every two iterations performs best. The plot to the right compares the best LC-MEMENTO synchronization with a partition approach. The partition approach performs better, since at each iteration, it performs no extra data movement compared to the LC variant which updates the data on the CPU by flushing its cache. We anticipate, LC-MEMENTO could perform better with unbalanced graphs as utilization becomes an issue with fixed partitions.

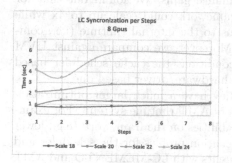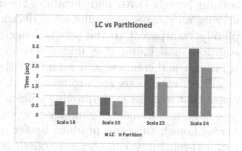

Fig. 9. LC-MEMENTO versus Partitioned BFS implementations

5 Related Work

Memory Consistency and Cache Coherency Protocols. [22] proposed a *hardware-assisted* cache coherency protocol for multi-GPU systems. In contrast, our approach is based on runtime software, with possibilities for expansion and integration of other consistency techniques. Recent proposals for sequential consistency include [11,21,23]. Although these works demonstrate that relaxed consistency protocols are no better than sequential consistency, our work shows that there can be considerable benefit for relaxed-synchronization based memory consistency models for select data analytics applications.

Scheduling Techniques. Recent works like MAPA [20], WOTIR [19], Gandiva [31] and Philly [12] explored placement optimizations of DNN workloads on multi-node multi-GPU environments. In Effisha [6], the authors proposed a preemptive scheduler for kernels to better support priority-based scheduling. Furthermore, Works like [1,2,26], explored hardware optimizations and require compiler-assisted code transformation and explicit insertion of runtime API calls in the original code. In contrast, our approach is transparent to runtime-assisted scheduling.

Programming Models. Groute [4] and Kokkos [27] proposed asynchronous multi-GPU programming models. However, memory consistency and ownership is required to be managed by the programmer in the aforementioned models. LC-MEMENTO, on the other hand, implements the location consistency memory model in the runtime and supports asynchronous execution in the runtime without programmer intervention.

6   Conclusions and Future Work

This paper presents the LC-MEMENTO extensions for an AMT runtime system. It allows the exploitation of current multi GPU designs with a transparent scheduler and a weaker memory models, instantiated as GPU cache with polymorphic synchronization/collective operators. These extensions were used to implement three kernels and showcased their performance gains. We found out that for certain kernels (with high locality) the framework could scale up to 4x while leaving all the resource allocation decisions to the internal runtime (i.e., completely transparent to the programmer). Moreover, we compare against UVM solutions and found that under certain conditions the cache/scheduler based solution could compete and even beat the hardware/driver based one.

These extensions are promising but they have a much larger optimization space that remains for improving efficiency of AMT runtime systems. For example, new enhancements to unlock new capabilities on the framework (e.g., lower kernel launch time can produce better execution profiles for the scheduler and faster throughput) can offer synergistic benefits with LC-MEMENTO and AMT runtime systems in general.

References

1. Abdolrashidi, A., et al.: WIREFRAME: supporting data-dependent parallelism through dependency graph execution in GPUs. In: Proceedings of the 50th Annual IEEE/ACM International Symposium on Microarchitecture, pp. 600–611 (2017)
2. Abdolrashidi, A., et al.: BlockMaestro: enabling programmer-transparent task-based execution in GPU systems. In: 2021 48th Annual IEEE/ACM International Symposium on Computer Architecture (ISCA). IEEE (2021)
3. Adve, S.V., Gharachorloo, K.: Shared memory consistency models: a tutorial. Computer **29**(12), 66–76 (1996)
4. Ben-Nun, T., et al.: Groute: an asynchronous multi-GPU programming model for irregular computations. ACM SIGPLAN Notices **52**(8), 235–248 (2017)
5. Bershad, B.N., Zekauskas, M.J.: Midway: shared memory parallel programming with entry consistency for distributed memory multiprocessors. Technical report (1991)
6. Chen, G., et al.: EffiSha: a software framework for enabling effficient preemptive scheduling of GPU. In: Proceedings of the 22nd ACM SIGPLAN Symposium on Principles and Practice of Parallel Programming, pp. 3–16 (2017)
7. Droco, M., et al.: Global Memory and Threading (GMT). https://github.com/pnnl/gmt
8. Firoz, J.S., Zalewski, M., Kanewala, T., Lumsdaine, A.: Synchronization-avoiding graph algorithms. In: 2018 IEEE 25th International Conference on High Performance Computing (HiPC), pp. 52–61. IEEE (2018)

9. Modelado Foundation: Open Community Runtime. https://xstackwiki.modelado. org/Open_Community_Runtime

10. Gao, G.R., Sarkar, V.: Location consistency-a new memory model and cache consistency protocol. IEEE Trans. Comput. **49**(8), 798–813 (2000)

11. Hechtman, B.A., Sorin, D.J.: Exploring memory consistency for massively-threaded throughput-oriented processors. In: Proceedings of the 40th Annual International Symposium on Computer Architecture, pp. 201–212 (2013)

12. Jeon, M., et al.: Analysis of large-scale multi-tenant GPU clusters for DNN training workloads. In: 2019 USENIX Annual Technical Conference (USENIX ATC 19), pp. 947–960 (2019)

13. Landwehr, J., et al.: Designing scalable distributed memory models: a case study. In: Proceedings of the Computing Frontiers Conference, CF 2017, pp. 174–182. Association for Computing Machinery, New York (2017)

14. Lenoski, D., et al.: The directory-based cache coherence protocol for the DASH multiprocessor. In: Proceedings of the 17th Annual International Symposium on Computer Architecture, ISCA 1990, pp. 148–159. ACM, New York (1990)

15. Long, G., et al.: Location consistency model revisited: problem, solution and prospects. In: 2008 Ninth International Conference on Parallel and Distributed Computing, Applications and Technologies, pp. 91–98 (2008)

16. Lustig, D., et al.: A formal analysis of the NVIDIA PTX memory consistency model. In: Proceedings of the Twenty-Fourth International Conference on Architectural Support for Programming Languages and Operating Systems, ASPLOS 2019, pp. 257–270. Association for Computing Machinery, New York (2019)

17. Luszczek, P.R., et al.: The HPC Challenge (HPCC) benchmark suite. In: Proceedings of the 2006 ACM/IEEE Conference on Supercomputing, SC 2006, p. 213-es. Association for Computing Machinery, New York (2006)

18. Protiae, J., Milutinoviae, V.: Entry consistency versus lazy release consistency in DSM systems: analytical comparison and a new hybrid solution. In: Proceedings of the Sixth IEEE Computer Society Workshop on Future Trends of Distributed Computing Systems, 1997, pp. 78–83, October 1997

19. Ranganath, K., et al.: Speeding up collective communications through inter-GPU re-routing. IEEE Comput. Archit. Lett. **18**(2), 128–131 (2019)

20. Ranganath, K., et al.: MAPA: multi-accelerator pattern allocation policy for multi-tenant GPU servers. In: SC21: International Conference for High Performance Computing, Networking, Storage and Analysis. ACM (2021)

21. Ren, X., Lis, M.: Efficient sequential consistency in GPUs via relativistic cache coherence. In: 2017 IEEE International Symposium on High Performance Computer Architecture (HPCA), pp. 625–636. IEEE (2017)

22. Ren, X., Lustig, D., Bolotin, E., Jaleel, A., Villa, O., Nellans, D.: HMG: extending cache coherence protocols across modern hierarchical multi-GPU systems. In: 2020 IEEE International Symposium on High Performance Computer Architecture (HPCA), pp. 582–595. IEEE (2020)

23. Singh, A., Aga, S., Narayanasamy, S.: Efficiently enforcing strong memory ordering in GPUs. In: Proceedings of the 48th International Symposium on Microarchitecture, pp. 699–712 (2015)

24. Rennich, S.: Streams and Concurrency. https://developer.download.nvidia.com/ CUDA/training/StreamsAndConcurrencyWebinar.pdf

25. Suetterlein, J., et al.: The Abstract Runtime System: ARTS. https://github.com/ pnnl/ARTS

26. Tripathy, D., et al.: LocalityGuru: a PTX analyzer for extracting thread block-level locality in GPGPUs. In: Proceedings of the 15th IEEE/ACM International Conference on Networking, Architecture, and Storage (2021, To appear)

27. Trott, C.R., Edwards, H.C.: Kokkos: the C++ performance portability programming model. Technical report, Sandia National Lab. (SNL-NM), Albuquerque, NM, United States (2017)

28. Ueno, K., Suzumura, T.: Highly scalable graph search for the Graph500 benchmark. In: Proceedings of the 21st International Symposium on High-Performance Parallel and Distributed Computing, HPDC 2012, pp. 149–160. Association for Computing Machinery, New York (2012)

29. Vergara, M., et al.: Scaling the summit: deploying the world's fastest supercomputer. In: International Workshop on OpenPOWER for HPC (IWOPH 2019) (2019)

30. Willcock, J.J., et al.: AM++: a generalized active message framework. In: Proceedings of the 19th International Conference on Parallel Architectures and Compilation Techniques, PACT 2010, pp. 401–410. Association for Computing Machinery, New York (2010). https://doi.org/10.1145/1854273.1854323

31. Xiao, W., et al.: Gandiva: introspective cluster scheduling for deep learning. In: 13th USENIX Symposium on Operating Systems Design and Implementation (OSDI 2018), pp. 595–610 (2018)

The ORKA-HPC Compiler—Practical OpenMP for FPGAs

Florian Mayer[1]([⊠]), Julian Brandner[1], Matthias Hellmann[2], Jesko Schwarzer[3], and Michael Philippsen[1]

[1] Programming Systems Group, Friedrich-Alexander University Erlangen-Nürnberg (FAU), Erlangen, Germany
{florian.andrefranc.mayer,julian.brandner,michael.philippsen}@fau.de
[2] Regional Computing Centre (RRZK), University of Cologne, Cologne, Germany
hellmann@uni-koeln.de
[3] Systemberatung Schwarzer, Cologne, Germany
orka-hpc@schwarzers.de

Abstract. ORKA-HPC is a new and downloadable OpenMP-to-FPGA compiler that is easy to set up, easy to use, and easy to extend. It targets a variety of different FPGA-boards, and is distributed with a "batteries included" runtime and development environment.

Starting from a set of properties that such a compiler must possess, we derive how ORKA-HPC achieves these, reason about the underlying decisions, and evaluate ORKA-HPC's current state of development. The paper concludes with future work and provides a download link.

1 Motivation

While some research groups attempted to build OpenMP-to-FPGA compilers [10], none of them made it into wide-spread use. Without commercial interest by industry, research funding often only suffices for building prototypes that address the posed research question but does not make the project's software valuable for other research groups. Even if there is open source code, it is hardly useful once the PhD students have left or the funding has ended. The ORKA-HPC OpenMP-to-FPGA compiler tries to avoid this fate by avoiding the following common mistakes and showstoppers.

1) Cross-Platform Issues. While mainstream programs are a part of a Linux distribution and available as pre-built binaries, research software in general does not make it into Linux distributions. Hence, there is only the source code plus instructions on how to compile and build. Interested parties thus have to ensure every build-time dependency, often by having to install specific versions of other tools or libraries. As sometimes the authors did not properly document all the dependencies, this makes it even harder to achieve a successful installation and thus to reproduce published results. In contrast, ORKA-HPC is easy to install on different Linux platforms and avoids dependency issues.

2) Shifting Grounds Issues. Where well-funded Linux distributions provide a stable execution environment with fixed APIs and libraries for a long time,

X. Li and S. Chandrasekaran (Eds.): LCPC 2021, LNCS 13181, pp. 83–97, 2022.
https://doi.org/10.1007/978-3-030-99372-6_6

84 F. Mayer et al.

others change more rapidly. Projects that are under active development can adapt their build- and run-time dependencies to such changes. However, once developers have left a project, their code often stops working after a short while. ORKA-HPC employs techniques to enhance its lifetime.

In Sect. 4 we discuss how ORKA-HPC achieves these general goals (portable cross-platform distribution and longevity). In addition, there are goals for FPGA projects and for compiler projects.

3) Stand on the Shoulders of Giants. To use an FPGA one needs to synthesize a Bitstream that describes the FPGA hardware. In general, special compilers (1) produce a tree representation for a C/C++ input, (2) generate an intermediate representation (IR), (3) optimize it, (4) generate a VHDL/Verilog hardware description from it, and (5) use a VHDL compiler to produce the Bitstream. Since FPGA vendors typically keep their hardware architectures undisclosed, little can be done in step 5 (hardware synthesis). In the past, researchers often reinvented all or some of the steps 1–4 (High-Level Synthesis, HLS). However, they were in competition with the vendors' industry-grade HLS tools and their developers. The ORKA-HPC compiler only builds crucial components from scratch and makes use of the best performing industry tools for both HLS and hardware synthesis.

4) Do Not Put all the Eggs in One Basket. Published OpenMP-to-FPGA compilers often generate FPGA hardware for one specific FPGA board. However, there are two issues here. First, different FPGA architectures are good for different computing tasks. Second, specific FPGA boards quickly become outdated. Hence, the ORKA-HPC compiler is extensible/portable for new devices and benefits from future advances of FPGA hardware. For the same reason the ORKA-HPC compiler is agnostic with respect to the board vendors. While APIs, options for both the HLS and the hardware synthesis, pipeline feedback, etc. are often at least upwards compatible for all the boards of a specific vendor, ORKA-HPC needs extra layers to gloss over differences between vendor tools.

Finally, there are goals for any research compiler, independent of targeting FPGAs. It must be **(5) easy to use** ideally as a drop-in replacement for Clang/GCC without modifications to the build system and it must be **(6) easy to extend** with regards to its internals. It is written in a way that it minimizes the effort to change the internals or to add new analysis/optimization algorithms.

In Sect. 3 we show how ORKA-HPC achieves these goals (reuse of optimized components as building blocks, retargetability to various FPGA types and brands, ease of use, and extensibility). Sect. 5 reports on some experiments to demonstrate that ORKA-HPC is operational.

2 Related Work

We discuss works mentioned in the survey by Mayer et al. [10], but exclude approaches that either require extensive hardware development knowledge (e.g. [2]), or that do not focus on offloading the OpenMP `target` pragma to the FPGA (e.g. [15]) but map other constructs.

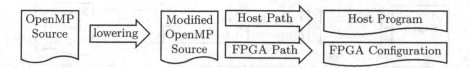

Fig. 1. Bird's eye view of ORKA-HPC's compilation process.

Bosch et al. [1] conduct target offloading for a programming model that is partially derived from OpenMP. They generate hardware from an annotation scheme closely resembling OpenMP's task based parallelism.

Sommer et al. [16] extract target regions and pass them to the TaPaSCo LLP backend. While being conceptually similar to ORKA-HPC, the tool is restricted to said backend and thereby inherits its platform dependencies.

In contrast to the above mentioned works (including ORKA-HPC) Knaust et al. [7] achieve offloading by passing an IR representation of the input region to a vendor tool. While providing a remarkably simple workflow, the method comes with a significant drawback, as it relies on an undocumented interface of one specific vendor tool.

Huthmann et al. [5] also use IR-level representations for Bitstream generation. But instead of passing them to commercially available tools their system explores the possibilities of using an open academic HLS infrastructure for target offloading. In contrast, ORKA-HPC exploits highly optimized vendor tools.

Nepomuneco et al. [12] focus on multi-FPGA environments and evaluate their speedups for just one specific accelerator platform.

To the best of our knowledge, none of the published systems gives details on how to achieve portability across Linux platforms, how to achieve longevity, how to exploit optimized tools as building blocks, how to target various brands and types of FPGA boards, and how to achieve ease of use and extensibility. ORKA-HPC tries to stay as accessible as your command line operated C compiler.

3 The ORKA-HPC OpenMP-to-FPGA Compiler

Here we introduce the building blocks of the ORKA-HPC compiler. We discuss the general architecture, the design options, and the reasons for ORKA-HPC's choices to achieve the goals above. We discuss distribution issues in Sect. 4.

The bird's eye view of the ORKA-HPC compiler in Fig. 1 shows its main processing paths and intermediate results. After lowering the OpenMP pragmas in the input source down to an intermediate form at a lower level of abstraction, the compiler then processes the modified OpenMP code by two distinct tool chains: An FPGA path offloads work to one or more FPGA devices and a host path generates the main program that manages the distribution of work.

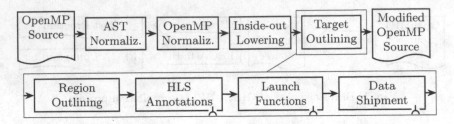

Fig. 2. AST-level OpenMP lowering. Hooks to plug in vendor-specific modules.

3.1 OpenMP Lowering

Which Pragmas to Offload to the FPGA? When building an OpenMP-to-FPGA compiler one has to decide which OpenMP pragmas to leave unchanged and to forward to a regular OpenMP compiler for a (shared memory) CPU (i.e., the host path), and which pragmas to transform so that the affected source code turns into FPGA hardware. By leaving pragmas for the host path that were designed for shared-memory systems with operating systems that provide the necessary synchronization primitives one can tap the general purpose compiler's optimization capabilities. There have been attempts to map OpenMP's synchronization primitives and shared-memory behavior to FPGAs, but they never matured beyond the proof-of-concept state, probably because there is a too wide gap between the fundamentally different computation models of FPGAs and CPUs. For instance, FPGAs neither permit easy thread synchronization nor access to the same shared memory of the CPU. For these reasons, ORKA-HPC only offloads the OpenMP `target` and `target data` pragmas to the FPGA and lowers pragmas that are nested inside the regions that both pragmas annotate.

How to Lower? In general, compilers (1) convert their input to an Abstract Syntax Tree (AST), (2) transform this AST, (3) map/lower the AST to a simpler intermediate representation (IR), and (4) generate assembly from it. Adding OpenMP support to an existing compiler requires additional AST node types and extensions to the steps 1, 2, and maybe 3. Compiler writers have two choices. First, they can replace all new OpenMP nodes with bundles of regular AST nodes. This so-called AST-level lowering only affects steps 1 and 2. Second, they can translate OpenMP nodes to intermediate form, just like all other AST nodes. This so-called AST-to-IR lowering also requires work on step 3.

ORKA-HPC uses an AST-level lowering and here is why: Offloading must transform a pragma into calls of runtime library functions that control the FPGA. On AST-level this is as simple as adding a function call node to the AST. After the transformation, the AST still represents regular C/C++ and can – after some pretty-printing – be fed into any vendor's HLS systems.

In contrast, AST-to-IR lowering has three problems. First, it needs the HLS system to be usable on IR-level but until lately [7], Intel's or Xilinx's HLS systems did only accept C/C++ inputs. Of course, the lowering could generate IR, optimize it, and convert it back to C/C++, but it is hard to decompile IR which is why LLVM for example has removed support for it in an early version [9]. Thus, OpenMP Fortran cannot yet be run on FPGAs, as this either requires IR-capable HLS systems or IR decompilers. Today, the situation seems to be a bit better as Vivado's HLS is now open source. Second, it requires an OpenMP runtime library in IR format (a set of IR-level routines) that have to be created somehow. Third, the AST-to-IR approach potentially inherits implementation details of vendor tool chains (e.g., the LLVM IR version that the tools support) which makes it hard to support multiple vendors and their FPGA boards [21].

Lowering Details. Figure 2 zooms into the first arrow in Fig. 1. To make an OpenMP-to-FPGA compiler easy to extend, both normalization steps are mandatory. Moreover, nested pragmas need to be lowered inside-out. Finally, to benefit from proven compiler tooling, existing generic outliners can be adjusted to work with separate memory domains. The following paragraphs explain the details.

AST Normalization. When an AST is first constructed from an input program, it often reflects the syntactic sugar that the programmer has used. For example, there are if-statements with a missing else branch or with an empty block; there are variable declarations with or without an initialization to the default value; there are for statements with a single statement in their bodies (for() s();) or with a block that holds the same statement (for(){s();}). Even though the semantics are the same, the AST representations differ and the compiler would need different cases in all its steps. It is thus common practice to normalize the AST before processing it. For example, branches of an if can always be turned into blocks of statements, variable declarations can always have an explicit initialization, etc. This cuts down on the number of cases in all compiler steps downstream and makes them easier to extend. The ORKA-HPC compiler follows this common practice and first reduces the complexity of the input AST.

```
#pragma omp target
#pragma omp teams
#pragma omp parallel
#pragma omp for
// equal to
#pragma omp target teams
#pragma omp parallel
#pragma omp for
// equal to
#pragma omp target teams
#pragma omp parallel for
```

Fig. 3. Combined pragmas.

OpenMP Normalization. OpenMP Normalization simplifies the AST w.r.t. OpenMP pragmas and makes an OpenMP-to-FPGA compiler easier to extend. The idea again is to normalize the input to a single representation that has all the default values set explicitly to avoid special cases for syntactic variants that have the same semantics.

In OpenMP several pragmas may or may not be combined. An example is target teams parallel for [14]. As illustrated in Fig. 3, the same can also be expressed in four lines with one pragma each, or in fewer code lines that hold two or more of these four pragmas. In essence, the combined form is a concatenation of the pragmas retaining their original order. The ORKA-HPC compiler brings all pragmas into an expanded normal form according to the rules of OpenMP. This yields fewer cases and reduces the complexity of writing the compiler and hence make it easier to extend.

Similar to a variable declaration that receives an explicit initialization to a default value when the programmer has not specified a different value, OpenMP normalization also adds default values to the AST nodes. Defaults are specified for most optional OpenMP clauses. Later on, the compiler can lower an AST node without knowing about default values. This separation of concerns is common practice applied to OpenMP translation.

```
// original code:
int a[];
{ /* code that uses a */ }
// after outlining:
int a[];
out(&a);
void out(int **a) {
  /* code that uses *a */
}
```

Fig. 4. Standard outlining.

Target Outlining. An OpenMP-to-FPGA compiler must partition the original program to offload parts of it to an FPGA. C-based HLS systems only accept entire C functions as input [6,19] and most HLS systems require these functions to be annotated with vendor specific pragmas or attributes. Moreover, the CPU code and the FPGA do not share memory.

Partitioning of programs for offloading is not new. OpenMP offloading for GPUs uses so-called outlining that wraps the piece of code under the target pragma in a new function and replaces the original region with a call of this function. ORKA-HPC strives to not reinvent the wheel. Instead of starting from a GPU outliner, as they are tailored to the demands of GPU vendor tool chains, it starts from a generic AST-level outliner that, however, is meant for a shared-memory situation. Figure 4 illustrates what a generic outliner would do. All the data that an outlined block of code accesses is passed to the outlined function as a set of pointers, i.e., with one level of indirection. This works well as long as caller and callee can access the same shared memory, but on an FPGA pointers to data in the host memory are meaningless, the HLS synthesis in general cannot handle them.

The ORKA-HPC compiler therefore extends a generic outliner with an address space cleanup that replaces infeasible pointer indirections with API calls that access the data in the other address space, depending on what the programmer has specified in the map clauses. See *Data Shipment* in Fig. 2.

Since the outlined function cannot simply be called after the synthesis turned it into FPGA hardware, the ORKA-HPC outliner inserts API calls to *ship data* to and from the FPGA and to *launch* the function's hardware. To achieve portability across different board types and vendors, the launch and the shipment APIs are generic. Most HLS systems require function annotations or special pragmas to produce valid and well-performing hardware. Despite the vendor-specific demands, the ORKA-HPC compiler still achieves portability by bundling the insertion of these annotations into another pluggable module, specific for each vendor but hidden behind a generic *annotation* API.

Inside-Out Lowering. So far we assumed that there was no nested pragma in a `target` region. To limit the engineering effort and to make the ORKA-HPC compiler easy to extend for new pragmas, it is best to process nested pragmas inside-out. At the deepest nesting level, a pragma only affects a region of plain, pragma-free code. At the deepest level, a pragma can be lowered without special cases for enclosed pragmas because there are none. To understand that such special cases are problematic, think of a target region that uses the variable a. If there can still be inner pragmas like for instance `parallel shared(a)`, the target outlining would need special cases for different flavors of variables. By lowering the pragmas inside-out, compiler writers only need to reason about one lowering template per pragma. Such a template replaces the code block affected by the pragma with a pragma-free code block. In the example, the `shared(a)` is long gone, when the outliner works on the `target` region. Inside-out lowering also eases experiments with research pragmas, as they can be lowered in isolation (as any potentially nested pragmas will already have been transformed away). Note that by climbing up the nesting levels of pragmas, the generated replacement code may be modified repeatedly, once per pragma layer.

To see why inside-out lowering works for non-trivial pragma situations, consider that in general a pragma only affects the statement or the scope directly below it. Inside-out lowering cannot handle clauses that affect a preceding line, i.e., a parent note in the AST. We do not know of such pragmas or clauses but could handle them with a pre-processing pass that adds attributes to the AST before the inside-out transformation.

The compiler needs to reject pragma combinations that cannot be mapped to an FPGA (e.g. there cannot be a `target` pragma inside another `target` pragma). While this check is straightforward to implement as part of the inside-out transformation, an outside-in approach would require a full subtree traversal that queries the structure of the pragmas nested below.

3.2 FPGA Path

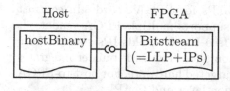

Fig. 5. LLP API.

According to Fig. 1, the OpenMP-to-FPGA compiler produces two artifacts geared to seamlessly work together. The FPGA must be configured to perform the offloaded work and the host program must make use of the FPGA, see Fig. 5. An FPGA is configured with a so-called Bitstream, i.e., a binary file that represents all the wires and logic gates of the circuit. In addition to these circuits that represent the offloaded function (called IP in FPGA lingo), it is common practice to capture infrastructure hardware in a so-called Low Level Platform (LLP). The LLP is used to interface with the host, e.g., via a PCIe interface, and it also contains the bus system to communicate with or among offloaded functions.

It is infeasible to generate these Bitstreams from scratch in the FPGA path, because the format of the Bitstream is proprietary. FPGA vendors typically

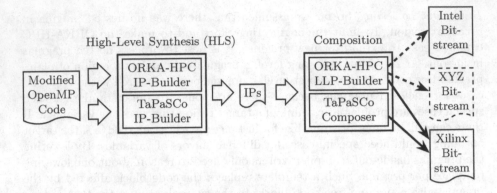

Fig. 6. FPGA path. Dashed means ongoing work.

provide hardware synthesis tools that offer many pre-built hardware blocks (e.g., for PCIe communication) and thus ease the development process. Such a tool is still impractical to use from a compiler, because it usually interprets a kind of abstract recipe to generate the Bitstream. For that reason LLP backends such as in ORKA-HPC or TaPaSCo [8] have been developed. As shown in Fig. 6, they get a set of C functions, build standalone hardware entities (IPs) for each of them, and write recipes that build an LLP plus IPs to form a fully functional FPGA. They also provide an LLP API to launch the execution of the work in the Bitstream from the host side, plus the necessary data shipment routines.

As these LLP backends are still mostly vendor specific, ORKA-HPC generalizes LLP functionality so that users can specify which LLP backend to use per `target` pragma. Different `target` regions can thus be offloaded to different FPGAs of a system. New LLP backends can also be added easily.

3.3   ORKA-HPC LLP-Backend

The ORKA-HPC LLP-backend provides LLPs for FPGA boards. In contrast to other such backends (like TaPaSCo), it supports multiple FPGA vendors. It consists of multiple parts: The IP-builder (see Fig. 6) builds IPs starting from the C-codes emitted by the ORKA-HPC compiler. The LLP-builder integrates these IPs and generates Bitstreams for the targeted hardware. For host-to-FPGA communication it also includes an abstraction layer and C API.

Tailored to the functionality and performance necessary for the ORKA-HPC compiler, the LLP-backend provides the tools necessary to generate Bitstreams and run OpenMP on FPGAs without any user input. While easily extendable in capability and fully configurable by the user, predefined and hand-optimized LLPs are provided for ease of use. With *partial reconfiguration* support, it allows for even more logic to be deployed on the FPGAs (sequentially) and reduces compile times. Its support of FPGAs from various vendors enables ORKA-HPC to distribute OpenMP workloads to a wide range of hardware configurations using one or multiple communication interfaces, including PCIe, Ethernet and

USB concurrently – a unique feature of ORKA-HPC not available in any other tool. In order to exploit the full potential of the FPGAs it internally uses the vendor's tool chains to generate IPs and Bitstreams. Since vendors typically update their tools alongside new hardware releases, this also facilitates adding compatibility to future devices and helps extend ORKA-HPC's lifetime.

The ORKA-HPC Generic Driver encapsulates device drivers and exposes a unified and vendor independent API for host-to-FPGA communication. FPGA selection can thus be done at runtime *on the fly* without the need to recompile library calls in the host binary, no matter which of the supported boards (brands) are targeted and how they are connected (e.g., locally via PCIe or *remotely* via TCP/IP). The *remote*-option is in fact a driver virtualization that enables driving FPGA boards through the internet or cloud solutions.

3.4 Host Path

We have discussed above that as part of the outlining, the ORKA-HPC compiler adds library calls to the host program that launch the offloaded functionality on the FPGA and that perform the data shipment to and from the FPGA. Because of its design goal to be useful for various types and brands of FPGAs, ORKA-HPC decouples the host binary both statically and dynamically from the various FPGA-specific LLPs. While decoupling is well known, to the best of our knowledge ORKA-HPC is the first tool that employs it that way.

For a static decoupling ORKA-HPC uses a generalized LLP API when lowering a `target` region. Adding a new type of FPGA to the ecosystem then only takes some glue code between the generalized LLP API and the concrete API.

For a dynamic decoupling ORKA-HPC loads concrete LLPs as plugins (at load-time) This allows to select an FPGA board per `target` region and it also allows to bind to a different LLP without recompiling the host code.

One particularly helpful LLP plugin in the ORKA-HPC environment is the Dummy LLP plugin. It only pretends to talk to an FPGA. In reality it executes every data shipment and IP control request locally and emulates the behaviour of the offloaded region on an FPGA. This eases and expedites the debugging of control messages as it saves the slow synthesis of FPGA hardware and drastically reduces the round-trip time (from hours to seconds).

ORKA-HPC therefore supports the use of a mixture of different LLPs in the *same* program and enables the host binary to switch between different LLPs, including the Dummy LLP, without recompilation. It is the latter feature that makes the ORKA-HPC compiler useful for LLP researchers as they can easily plug in experimental versions of their codes. To demonstrate the extensibility of the ORKA-HPC solution, we plugged in the TaPaSCo Composer [8] in addition to the ORKA-HPC LLP backend.

4 Deployment

For easy installation of a compiler on a variety of platforms, both the compiler and the build process for the compiler must run on different platforms. An

OpenMP-to-FPGA compiler is harder to get up and running than a regular C compiler as the former in general relies on specific versions of other components (e.g., LLP backend, FPGA tool chain, C compiler, etc.).

Well-known challenges of a portable build process are to manage the build-time dependencies and to ensure them on other systems. There are popular solutions that unfortunately limit the ease of using ORKA-HPC. First, using a Virtual Machine to distribute a piece of software is equivalent to shipping a 1:1 image of the developer's computer. The disadvantages are: The VM approach only works as long as the VM can be executed. There is almost no extensibility. In general, the size of such a VM is enormous (several gigabytes). Above all, team development is severely restricted, since a change of the VM requires a copy of the entire VM to be shipped to other team members. Second, dependency managers such as Nix [13] add complexities for both the developers and the build-process. Third, custom shell scripts that tailor each build environment to fit a given Linux distribution take effort to write and are hard to maintain.

ORKA-HPC avoids the above disadvantages by using Docker [3] for deployment. Instead of having to ship a 1:1 image, the ORKA-HPC compiler provides a small recipe, the so-called Dockerfile, that describes the Docker containers that act like Virtual Machines in which the specified environment for build- and runtime are set up correctly. Although we recommend the Docker tools to build the ORKA-HPC environment automatically from the Dockerfile, users can also simply follow those human-readable instructions to build ORKA-HPC themselves. Compiled programs also do not need the Docker container.

5   Evaluation

target
target data
target teams*
target distribute*
target teams distribute*
target parallel*
target parallel for*
target teams distribute simd*
target update
target enter data◇
target exit data◇
declare target
end declare target

Fig. 7. Supported OpenMP.

In this section we report on the current state of an ongoing project. We list the OpenMP pragmas that ORKA-HPC currently supports, give performance numbers on an embarrassingly parallel Mandelbrot experiment, and discuss the current functional completeness on a set of benchmarks that was never designed to be offloaded to FPGAs.

Pragma Coverage. Figure 7 lists all the pragmas that ORKA-HPC currently supports for FPGA offloading. ORKA-HPC only covers **target** pragmas or pragmas nested below them. The underlying generic OpenMP compiler deals with all other pragma situations. There are three caveats to Fig. 7. We correctly parse the combined **target** constructs marked with *, generate AST nodes, and normalize them; we do not yet exploit their

Table 1. Mandelbrot performance. Runtimes are given in milliseconds. The Xilinx VCU118 has the following resources available: $FF_{avail} = 2,364,480$. $LUT_{avail} = 1,182,240$. $DSP_{avail} = 6,840$. $BRAM_{avail} = 2,160$.

Unroll factor	1			8	32	64	128
Frequency	100 MHz	200 MHz	400 MHz	400 MHz	400 MHz	350 MHz	50 MHz
FF_{all}	6.09%	6.09%	6.09%	7.23%	11.06%	16.16%	26.36%
LUT_{all}	9.49%	9.49%	9.53%	10.44%	13.25%	17.11%	24.95%
DSP_{all}	0.57%	0.57%	0.57%	4.25%	16.89%	33.73%	67.41%
$BRAM_{all}$	5.19%	5.19%	5.19%	5.19%	5.19%	5.19%	5.19%
FF_{mandel}	5.3%	5.3%	5.3%	20.1%	47.8%	64.3%	78.1%
LUT_{mandel}	3.0%	3.0%	3.3%	11.7%	31.5%	47.3%	63.7%
DSP_{mandel}	92.3%	92.3%	92.3%	99.0%	99.7%	99.9%	99.9%
$BRAM_{mandel}$	2.2%	2.2%	2.2%	2.2%	2.2%	2.2%	2.2%
FPGA runtime	2592.0	1296.0	0648.0	0109.6	0033.4	**0023.0**	0102.8
transf. to/alloc	0000.8	0000.8	0000.8	0000.8	0000.8	0000.8	0000.8
transf. from	0003.6	0003.6	0003.6	0003.5	0003.6	0003.6	0003.6

semantics to generate efficient parallel FPGA structures, i.e., there is not yet an automatic mapping for instance of a `parallel for` to the HLS directives that would cause parallel FPGA hardware. For the pragmas marked with ◇ we do not yet emit the library routines. Finally, all translation units must be compiled with ORKA-HPC before linking. Kernels and library code compiled with other compilers cannot be called in target regions.

Mandelbrot Performance. We wrote a Mandelbrot code with an explicit loop unroll parameter to study the performance of the FPGAs that ORKA-HPC generates. Per unrolled loop iteration there is a sub-block of FPGA hardware that implements the loop body for a parallel execution. Our code first transfers *all* data to the FPGA, triggers the Mandelbrot calculation, and finally transfers back *all* the data. The first four rows of Table 1 show the overall utilization of our VCU118 FPGA board, according to the Vivado Bitstream synthesis report. The columns hold various unroll factors and FPGA clock frequencies. The rows report on the fraction of FlipFlop (FF), Look-up-tables (LUT), Digital Signal Processor (DSP) blocks, and BRAM modules of the full board that our generated IPs populate.[1] There are four rows that show the resource consumption for *all* components of the Bitstream, i.e., the LLP and the Mandelbrot IP. The *mandel* rows tell how much of those resources the Mandelbrot IP uses. The upper shaded area shows the significant fixed cost of the LLP plus one Mandelbrot IP. Unrolled versions of this IP amortize the LLP cost. The lower shaded area holds the cost

---

[1] A LUT can be configured to behave like an arbitrary n-to-1 logic function and FFs are usually grouped to resemble n-bit registers. Most high-end FPGAs provide DSP blocks as ASIC components to accelerate floating-point heavy tasks.

Table 2. Mandelbrot performance on CPUs.

Processor	Xeon		i7	
Num. threads	1	6	1	6
Runtime (secs.)	0.02451	**0.01872**	0.01184	**0.00634**
Std. deviation	0.00152	0.00376	0.00185	0.00096
Flags	-O3	-O3	-O3	-O3
		-fopenmp		-fopenmp
GCC version	7.5.0		7.5.0	

Xeon = Intel(R) Xeon(R) Gold 5220 CPU (2.20 GHz, 72 log. cores).
i7 = Intel(R) Core(TM) i7-4770 CPU (3,40 GHz, 8 log. cores).

of one Mandelbrot IP. There again are fixed costs plus variable unrolling costs for FF, LUT, etc. The variable costs have different growth rates as can be seen in the columns of the higher unroll factors.

The last three rows show our runtime performance measurements for each Bitstream. Here, we show the pure FPGA runtime, "transf. to/alloc" gives the time needed for the data shipment plus the allocation, and "transf. from" is the duration for the data to return. Shipping the full data to/from the FPGA is neither affected by the unroll factor nor by the FPGA's clock frequency. All runtime durations were calculated by timing measurement routines that ORKA-HPC automatically placed into the host binary. All durations given are the averages of ten independent runs of the same program on one Intel(R) Core(TM) i7-4770 CPU (clocked at 3.40 GHz, consisting of 8 logical cores). The standard deviations of all durations range from $1.08 \cdot 10^{-6}$ (min) and $4.49 \cdot 10^{-5}$ (max).

For the first three columns, we left the unroll factor fixed at 1 (i.e., one Mandelbrot IP) but varied the IP frequencies from 100 MHz to 400 MHz. As expected, the FPGA utilization did not change much, but the execution speed doubled each time we doubled the frequency. Our code did not meet hardware timing requirements for frequencies above 400 MHz. The next four columns show higher unroll factors and the maximal possible frequency (in multiples of 50 MHz). For instance, when the unroll factor is 8, our offloaded function fetches eight pixels from the memory of the VCU118 via a DMA transfer, processes each pixel in parallel, and writes 8 pixels back into the FPGA memory (also via DMA). The best execution speed for an unroll factor of 64 and a clock frequency of 350 MHz is in **bold** in Table 1. Unfortunately, for an unroll factor of 128, the code did not compile beyond 50 MHz due to hardware timing issues.

Table 2 shows the performance of the same Mandelbrot code on off-the-shelves computers without FPGAs. Since generic C compilers ignore the HLS pragmas, we added a `parallel for` pragma to the unrollable loop so that is can use six cores of our hardware. Our FPGA runtimes in Table 1 are about on par.

Table 3. Functional verification with SPEC ACCEL.

Benchmark stage	503. postencil	504. polbm	514. pomriq	552. pep	554. pcg	557. pcsp	570. pbt
Frontend	✓	✓	✓	✓	✓	_1	_1
Mock with dummy LLP	✓	✓	✓	✓	✓		
HLS for x functions	1✓	2✓ of 3^2	2✓	5✓	13✓ of 16^3		
FPGA	✓		✓	✓			
Time for Mock	6.13 s	18.26 s	4.23 s	11.71 s	19.91 s		
Time for HLS	55.21 s	119.81 s	102.56 s	314.21 s	967.87 s		
Time for FPGA	7065.63 s		6928.39 s	9836.89 s			

[1] Uses the `[:]`-Syntax in a map clause which we do not yet support.
[2] One offloaded function used a pointer cast that the HLS does not support.
[3] HLS aborts with unknown error for three offloaded functions.

Multi-board Support. The Mandelbrot code runs on multiple boards. We can configure ORKA-HPC to pick the ORKA-HPC LLP backend for the Arty board [11]. For the Vivado VCU118 [20] board, we can pick both the ORKA-HPC and the TaPaSCo LLP backend. Data transfers to/from the Arty board happen via Ethernet. The communication with the VCU118 uses the PCIe interface.

SPEC ACCEL. We used ORKA-HPC with the seven unmodified SPEC ACCEL benchmarks [17] that employ target offloading. Only for 514.pomriq we had to manually expand `#include "computeQ.c"` to fix a pre-processor issue. The benchmarks are not meant to be used with FPGA offloading as they use **floats** or **doubles** which is not among the strength of FPGAs as the HLS synthesis of standard C floating point data types takes up considerable amounts of resources [4]. This is why this section is only a report on the functionality of ORKA-HPC, not on the performance gained.

Table 3 is a work-in-progress report. Its upper part illustrates the current state of the ORKA-HPC pipeline at the time of writing this paper. For each of the seven benchmarks it shows which stage of the compilation it successfully passes. The Frontend stage includes all ORKA-HPC steps that transform the input code into a host binary that can interact with an FPGA via different LLP backends. The footnotes show the current limitations. Codes that pass the Mock stage run with the Dummy LLP plugin that simulates an FPGA. They produce the same results as a host-only compilation without `-fopenmp`. A check mark in the HLS row tells that we can successfully translate the offloaded functions to hardware blocks. For two benchmarks there are issues in Vivado HLS 2018.2 that prevent synthesis for 1 or 3 functions. A newer version of Vivado's HLS fixes some of these bugs, but at the time of writing we still have to migrate to it. The FPGA row reports on a successful generation of the full Bitstream.

In the lower part of Table 3 we show how long the pipeline phases take (wall clock time) on a Intel(R) Xeon(R) Gold 5220 CPU (clocked at 2.20 GHz, consisting of 72 logical cores) with 496 GB of available RAM. As we are actively working on the benchmarks, the table will have more ✓ in the final version.

At the time being, the benchmarks that run with FPGAs are not as fast as CPU-only versions. (And because of the floating point computations they cannot be expected to.) The runtimes can be off by a factor of up to 900. We identified the top two reasons. First, we currently neither automatically generate an explicit unrolling nor the pragmas that would tell the HLS where to use parallel hardware. The Mandelbrot experiment shows the importance of this. Second, the HLS generates an independent memory request to an off-chip RAM for *every* array access, without any caching. Adding suitable HLS pragmas for this is also in our future work.

6   Contributions and Future Work

We contribute ORKA-HPC, a new OpenMP compiler for FPGAs that has several novel properties. First, it is portable across different Linux platforms and uses Docker to ease the build process (of the compiler) despite of version updates in the infrastructure tools. Second, ORKA-HPC is designed to reuse many optimized building blocks provided by vendors while also hiding vendor-specific details behind APIs. This enables ORKA-HPC to use various types and brands of FPGAs. Third, AST-level transformations that lower pragmas inside-out (after some normalizations) make it easy to add support for more pragmas and to hide low-level compiler construction details. Therefore, ORKA-HPC lowers the bar for future FPGA-based OpenMP research. The ORKA-HPC distribution – including all sources and benchmarks[2] – is available from https://github.com/ORKA-HPC/orkadistro

Currently, we are working on two main issues. First, as they can drastically decrease the resource consumption on FPGAs, we make bit-accurate data types available for programmers [4]. Second, because offloading unmodified C code to an FPGA in general does not lead to well-performing hardware, we automatically insert and tune HLS annotations to improve resource utilization on FPGAs.

Acknowledgments. The authors acknowledge the financial support by the Federal Ministry of Education and Research of Germany in the framework of ORKA-HPC (project numbers 01IH17003C and 01IH17003A). We also thank Marius Knaust (Zuse Institute Berlin, ZIB) for recommending the SPEC ACCEL benchmark and the ROSE team for the ROSE [18] framework with its OpenMP 3.0 lowering support.

References

1. Bosch, J., et al.: Application acceleration on FPGAs with OmpSs@FPGA. In: Proceedings of the International of Conference on Field-Programmable Technology, FPT 2018, Naha, Japan, December 2018, pp. 70–77 (2018)
2. Ceissler, C., Nepomuceno, R., Pereira, M.M., Araujo, G.: Automatic offloading of cluster accelerators. In: Proceedings of the International Symposium on Field-Programmable Custom Computing Machines, FCCM 208, Boulder, CO, April 2018 p. 224 (2018)
3. Docker Inc.: Docker. https://www.docker.com. Accessed 29 Sept 2021

---

[2] We do not include the SPEC ACCEL benchmarks as they require a SPEC license.

4. Finnerty, A., Ratigner, H.: Reduce power and cost by converting from floating point to fixed point (March 2017). https://www.xilinx.com/support/documentation/white_papers/wp491-floating-to-fixed-point.pdf. Accessed 29 Sept 2021
5. Huthmann, J., Sommer, L., Podobas, A., Koch, A., Sano, K.: OpenMP device offloading to FPGAs using the Nymble infrastructure. In: Proceedings of the International Workshop On OpenMP, IWOMP 2020, Austin, TX, September 2020, pp. 265–279 (2020)
6. Intel Corporation: Intel Quartus Prime. https://www.intel.com/content/www/us/en/software/programmable/quartus-prime/hls-compiler.html. Accessed 29 Sept 2021
7. Knaust, M., Mayer, F., Steinke, T.: OpenMP to FPGA offloading prototype using OpenCL SDK. In: Proceedings of the International Workshop on High-Level Parallel Programs, Models and Supportive Environment, HIPS 2019, Rio de Janeiro, Brazil, May 2019, pp. 387–390 (2019)
8. Korinth, J., Hofmann, J., Heinz, C., Koch, A.: The TaPaSCo open-source Toolflow for the automated composition of task-based parallel reconfigurable computing systems. In: Proceedings of the International Symposium on Applied Reconfigurable Computing, ARC 2019, Darmstadt, Germany, April 2019, pp. 214–229 (2019)
9. LLVM Team: LLVM 3.1 Release Notes. https://releases.llvm.org/3.1/docs/ReleaseNotes.html. Accessed 29 Sept 2021
10. Mayer, F., Knaust, M., Philippsen, M.: OpenMP on FPGAs-a survey. In: Proceedings of the International Workshop On OpenMP, IWOMP 2019, Auckland, New Zealand, August 2019, pp. 94–108 (2019)
11. National Instruments Corporation: Artix-7 FPGA Development Board. https://reference.digilentinc.com/reference/programmable-logic/arty/start. Accessed 29 Sept 2021
12. Nepomuceno, R., Sterle, R., Valarini, G., Pereira, M., Yviquel, H., Araujo, G.: Enabling OpenMP task parallelism on multi-FPGAs. arXiv arXiv:2103.10573 [cs.DC] (March 2021)
13. NixOS Contributors: Nix. https://nixos.org. Accessed 29 Sept 2021
14. OpenMP architecture review board: device data environments. https://www.openmp.org/wp-content/uploads/OpenMP-API-Specification-5.0.pdf. Accessed 29 Sept 2021
15. Podobas, A., Brorsson, M.: Empowering OpenMP with automatically generated hardware. In: Proceedings of the International Conference on Systems, Architectures, Modeling and Simulation, SAMOS 2016, Agios Konstantinos, Greece, January 2016, pp. 245–252 (2016)
16. Sommer, L., Korinth, J., Koch, A.: OpenMP device offloading to FPGA accelerators. In: Proceedings of the International Conference on Application-Specific Systems, Architectures and Processors, ASAP 2017, Seattle, WA, July 2017, pp. 201–205 (2017)
17. SPEC: SPEC ACCEL. https://www.spec.org/accel/. Accessed 29 Sept 2021
18. The ROSE Team: ROSE Compiler. http://rosecompiler.org/. Accessed 29 Sept 2021
19. Xilinx: Vitis High-Level Synthesis. https://www.xilinx.com/html_docs/xilinx2021_1/vitis_doc/introductionvitishls.html. Accessed 29 Sept 2021
20. Xilinx Virtex UltraScale+ FPGA VCU118 Evaluation Kit. https://www.xilinx.com/products/boards-and-kits/vcu118.html. Accessed 29 Sept 2021
21. Xilinx: Xilinx Vitis HLS LLVM 2020.2. https://github.com/Xilinx/HLS. 29 Sept 2021

Graphs and Kernels

Optimizing Sparse Matrix Multiplications for Graph Neural Networks

Shenghao Qiu[1], Liang You[2], and Zheng Wang[1(✉)]

[1] University of Leeds, Leeds, UK
{sc19sq,z.wang5}@leeds.ac.uk
[2] Alibaba Group, Beijing, China
youliang.yl@alibaba-Inc.com

Abstract. Graph neural networks (GNNs) are emerging as a powerful technique for modeling graph structures. Due to the sparsity of real-world graph data, GNN performance is limited by extensive sparse matrix multiplication (SpMM) operations involved in computation. While the right sparse matrix storage format varies across input data, existing deep learning frameworks employ a single, static storage format, leaving much room for improvement. This paper investigates how the choice of sparse matrix storage formats affect the GNN performance. We observe that choosing a suitable sparse matrix storage format can significantly improve the GNN training performance, but the right format depends on the input workloads and can change as the GNN iterates over the input graph. We then develop a predictive model to dynamically choose a sparse matrix storage format to be used by a GNN layer based on the input matrices. Our model is first trained offline using training matrix samples, and the trained model can be applied to any input matrix and GNN kernels with SpMM computation. We implement our approach on top of PyTorch and apply it to 5 representative GNN models running on a multi-core CPU using real-life and synthetic datasets. Experimental results show that our approach gives an average speedup of 1.17x (up to 3x) for GNN running time.

1 Introduction

In recent years, graph neural networks (GNNs) [46] are shown to be effective in extracting information from graph structures like social networks with millions of nodes and billions of edges [8]. Indeed, GNNs account for over 90% of the leading models in solving the open graph benchmark suite [16,17].

A GNN is designed to propagate and aggregate information across graph nodes. This is achieved by applying a kernel function to a feature matrix of graph nodes, which captures the properties of nodes, as well as an adjacency matrix that encodes the connectivity of graph edges. The kernel function is typically

---

Z. Wang—This project was supported in part by an Alibaba Innovative Research Programme.

X. Li and S. Chandrasekaran (Eds.): LCPC 2021, LNCS 13181, pp. 101–117, 2022.
https://doi.org/10.1007/978-3-030-99372-6_7

implemented using matrix multiplications [46] that often dominate the GNN execution time during training and inference. Because most of the nodes in a real-life graph only have a small number of direct neighbors, the graph adjacency matrix that a GNN kernel operates on is often sparse (i.e., many matrix elements are zeros). As a result, the matrix multiplication computation within a GNN is essentially sparse matrix multiplication (SpMM) operations.

There is an extensive body of work in optimizing SpMM for scientific workloads [13]. Various sparse matrix storage formats have been proposed to reduce the memory and computation overhead of SpMM [14,19]. Studies have also shown that choosing the right storage format can have a significant impact on the SpMM performance [21]. Although SpMM performance optimization is a well-studied field in traditional high-performance computing (HPC) domains, the benefit of sparse matrix storage format selection is unclear on the new GNN workloads. Existing deep learning frameworks like PyTorch [23] and Tensorflow [1] all use a single, static sparse matrix storage format across graph inputs. Since GNNs are becoming an important application class, it is essential to understand how GNN performance can benefit from sparse matrix format selection.

This paper presents the first study of sparse matrix storage selection on GNN performance. We consider five representative GNN architectures and six commonly used sparse matrix storage formats. We empirically demonstrate that choosing a suitable sparse matrix storage format can have a significant performance benefit, but the right format changes depending on the input matrix. We show that unlike traditional HPC workloads, the matrix sparsity can change over time as the GNN iterates over the input graph; and as a result, the suitable format can vary throughout GNN execution.

In light of this observation, we employ machine learning to automatically construct a predictive model based on XGBoost [7] for sparse matrix format selection. Our predictor predicts, at runtime, the sparse matrix storage format and the associate SpMM computation kernel for each GNN kernel. Our predictor is first trained *off-line* using synthetic matrix data. Then, using a set of automatically tuned features of the matrix input, the predictor determines the optimal storage format to use before entering a kernel. We showcase that our approach is generally applicable and can adapt to various optimization goals to find different trade-offs between the memory overhead and execution time.

We evaluate our approach by applying it to five GNN architectures running on multi-core CPUs using both real-life and synthetic graph data. We compare our approach against two prior machine-learning methods [24,27] for selecting sparse matrix storage formats. Experimental results show that our approach gives better performance over alternative optimization strategies by giving an average 1.17x speedup. The performance of our approach translates to average 89% of the oracle, a theoretically perfect predictor for storage form selection (Sect. 6.3) performance given by a theoretically perfect predictor.

This paper makes the following contributions:

– It is the first paper to study sparse matrix storage format selection on GNN performance;

- It shows how machine learning techniques can be employed to develop a runtime predictor for optimizing GNN sparse matrix format selection;
- It provides quantified performance results of widely used sparse matrix storage formats on representative GNN architectures.

2   Background

2.1   Graph Neural Networks

A GNN operates on a graph structure, where each graph node is associated with a d-dimensional feature vector of numerical values known as embeddings. Edges between nodes indicate their relationship, quantified with edge weights. For a graph with N nodes, the graph edges are encoded in an $N \times N$ adjacency matrix, A, and the node embeddings are stored in an $N \times d$ feature matrix, X.

Like most neural networks, a GNN model can have multiple layers. Each layer is represented by two functions: i) an aggregation function and ii) an update function (i.e., a combination function). During training, a GNN takes as input the adjacency matrix, A, of the graph. It then uses a neighbourhood aggregation scheme to update the feature vector of each graph node based on the feature vector of its neighboring nodes. Feature aggregation is performed by first applying the aggregation function (e.g., reductions) to collect the features of the neighbours for a given node and then updating each node's feature vectors using the updating function. After repeating this process of updating node features for a fixed number of times, a readout function is applied to aggregate the feature matrix to a single numerical vector to be used as the graph representation.

The aggregation and update functions used by a GNN layer are implemented using matrix multiplications. Because the graph adjacency matrix, A, is sparse in many real-life graphs, the GNN matrix multiplications are often realized as SpMM to reduce the memory footprint and processing time [17]. When profiling 5 representative GNN models (Sect. 5.1) on real-life datasets, we find that SpMM can account for 95% of the GNN processing time.

2.2   Sparse Matrix Storage Formats

Our work considers the following commonly used sparse matrix storage formats:

COO. The coordinate list (COO) stores a list of (row, column, value) tuples of non-zero elements. This is the default storage format used by PyTorch-geometric [11] for graph processing.

CSR. The compressed sparse row (CSR) format uses three arrays to represent non-zero matrix elements, that respectively contain non-zero values, the beginning position of each row, and the column indices of non-zero elements. CSR is similar to COO, but compresses the row indices, hence the name.

CSC. The compressed sparse column format (CSC) is similar to CSR, with one exception for using an array to store the target matrix's row indices of non-zero elements instead of column indices as in CSR.

Table 1. Input matrix sparsity from graph datasets

Name	Adj. Matrix Density	Adj. Matrix Size	Node Feature Vector Dimension
CoraFull	0.6%	$19,793 \times 8,710$	19,793
Cora	1.27%	$2,708 \times 1,433$	2,708
DblpFull	0.31%	$17,716 \times 1,639$	17,716
PubmedFull	10.02%	$19,717 \times 500$	19,717
KarateClub	2.94%	34×34	34

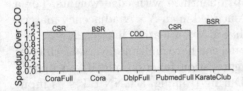

Fig. 1. The best-performing storage format per dataset.

Fig. 2. Changes of the adjacency matrix density over GNN training epochs.

DIA. The diagonal format (DIA) stores non-zero elements along the diagonal direction of a matrix into a row of a 2-dimensional array. It is best suited for non-zero elements that appear along the diagonals of a matrix.

BSR. The block sparse row format (BSR) evenly divides the input matrix into blocks. It is CSR with dense sub-matrices of fixed shape instead of scalar items.

DOK. The dictionary of keys format (DOK) stores key-value pairs <(row,column), value> in a dictionary (e.g., a hash table). Elements that are not presented in the dictionary are treated as zero elements.

LIL. The linked list (LIL) format stores non-zero elements and their column indices in a linked list. This format uses a row-based linked list, where each row is a list of column indices of non-zero elements.

3 Motivation

As a motivating example, consider applying a two-layered graph convolution network (GCN) model [18] to 5 real-life graph datasets (Table 1) using the 7 sparse matrix storage formats described in Sect. 2.2.

3.1 Setup

In this experiment, we consider five real-life graph datasets used in prior work [2]. Table 1 summarizes the size and sparsity of the graph adjacency matrix, and the dimension of the node feature vector (a dense vector). We run the GCN model on a 2.0 GHz 20-core Intel Xeon CPU. We note that it is common to run a GNN on the CPU due to the large memory footprint of graph processing [2].

3.2 Results

Figure 1 shows the best-performing sparse matrix format for each dataset, when a format is used to encode the initial model input and used throughout the model training process. Here, we normalize the measured runtime against the time of the PyTorch-geometric default COO format. While COO gives the best performance on `DBLPFull`, it leaves much room for performance improvement on other datasets. Furthermore, we also observe that the best-performing storage format varies depending on the input dataset.

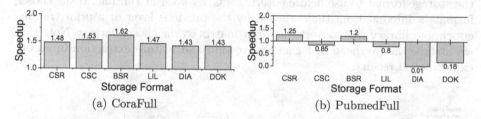

(a) CoraFull   (b) PubmedFull

Fig. 3. Performance improvement over the PyTorch-geometric default COO format on the CoraFull (a) and PubmedFull dataset (b) when using different sparse matrix format to store the output of the first GNN layer.

If we now consider Fig. 2, we see that the density of the input matrix increases as we iterate over the GNN model on the `CoraFull` dataset. This is expected as a GNN tries to incorporate further neighbourhood information by iterating over the graph, which in turn increases the reach and information propagation of a graph node. As can be seen in Fig. 3, CSR is the best format used to store the neural network input (i.e., the feature and the adjacency matrix) for both the `CoraFull` and `PubmedFull` datasets. Thus, for a model with a single layer GNN, CSR might be the best storage format. However, for a typical GNN model with multiple GNN layers, the sparsity of the matrices processed by the latter layers can change, calling for a different storage format to be used. Specifically, for `CoraFull` (Fig. 3(a)) used in our setting, using CSC, LIL and DIA after the first GNN layer can also give a relatively good speedup over COO, but these format give no benefit on `PubmedFull` (Fig. 3(b)) because of the changing distribution of the non-zero elements, the details can be seen in Fig. 3.

Lesson learned. This example shows that choosing the right sparse matrix storage format can have a significant performance benefit, but the choice depends on the input data and the GNN layers. Therefore, the decision for storage format should be made on a per GNN layer basis during runtime.

4   Our Approach

Our work aims to choose the most efficient sparse matrix storage format for accelerating GNN performance or finding a trade-off between the memory footprint and runtime. As the right choice depends on the characteristics of the input matrix processed by a GNN layer, and the optimal storage format can change over the duration of the training, we wish to develop an approach to automatically derive a storage format (and the SpMM kernel) on a per input basis.

To this end, we employ machine learning to build a classifier to predict the sparse matrix storage format to use from a pool of candidate formats. The predictive model takes as input a feature vector of numerical values, which describe the essential characteristics of the input matrix. It then produces a label, indicating which of the storage formats to be used by a GNN layer. We provide APIs (Sect. 4.6) to monitor the input matrix sparsity and dynamically adjust the storage format to use before entering a GNN layer at runtime. If the chosen format is different from the one used by the previous layer or a prior training epoch, our library will convert the input matrix to the chosen format. Note that we include the overhead of format conversion and feature extraction in all our experimental results.

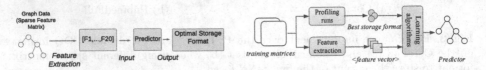

Fig. 4. Overview of our predictive model for choosing sparse matrix storage format.   **Fig. 5.** Overview of our training process

4.1   Predictive Modeling

Our predictive model builds upon the XGBoost classifier [7]. We have evaluated a number of alternative classification techniques, including multilayer perceptron (MLP) neural networks, K-Nearest neighbour (KNN), and support vector machines (SVM). We choose XGBoost because of its good generalization ability [7], its decision-tree-like structure is interpretable, and its better and more robust performance over alternatives on our problem (Sect. 6.4). In the remainder of this section, we describe our predictive model by following the classical 4-step process for supervised learning: i) problem modeling, ii) training data generation, iii) train a predictor and iv) implement the predictor.

4.2   Problem Modeling

Figure 4 depicts the workflow of our approach. The deployed model extracts features from the adjacency and feature matrices and uses the feature values to predict the sparse matrix storage format to use. Our library automatically converts the input matrix to the selected storage format if needed. Note that a SpMM computation kernel can be chosen based on the object type of the input. Since we implemented our prototype in PyTorch, this computation kernel selection process is performed automatically by the Python library.

As depicted in Fig. 5, our model is trained offline using training samples. The trained model can be applied to any previously unseen matrix. Training involves finding the best storage format, extracting feature values for each training matrix and learning a model from the training data, described as follows.

4.3   Training Data Generation

We use 300 synthetically generated square matrices to train the XGBoost model. The matrix size of our training samples ranges from $1,000$ to $15,000$, increased with a step of 200. We populate the matrix with random values of 0 and 1 with a sparsity ranging from 0.1% to 70%, to simulate the matrix sparsity seen at the initial model graph input and later message propagation stages. For each training matrix, we exhaustively execute the SpMM computation kernel with each sparse matrix storage format and record the best performing format for each matrix sample on each kernel. We then label each best-performing configuration with a unique number (i.e., class label). Note that we apply cross-validation in our evaluation to make sure we always test the trained model on unseen datasets.

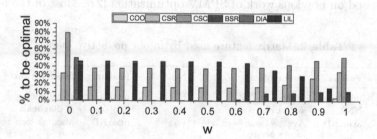

Fig. 6. How often a storage format is considered to be optimal on our synthetic training data when varying the weight w in Eq. 1. Noted that there might be multiple optimal formats for a single input if the final output O is very similar (± 0.0001).

Optimization Goal. Our approach allows the user to find a trade-off between the memory footprint and the GNN performance and train a predictive model for their optimization goal. Specifically, in this work, we consider the following optimization formulation, but other formulas can also be used:

$$\min_{O} O_{l \in L} = w \times R + (1.0 - w) \times M \tag{1}$$

where R and M are the normalized running time and memory footprint for a sparse matrix storage format from a collection of candidate formats (L), and w is a configurable weight parameter. Note that we scale the execution time and memory footprint to the $(0,1)$ range using the min-max values found from the profiled training data. Essentially, our goal is to minimize the weighted sum, O in Eq. 1 to trade runtime for a lower memory footprint. For example, setting w to 0 and 1.0 means we only optimize for memory overhead and speeds respectively.

Our training data includes the raw measurements of the execution time and memory footprint for each storage format under each matrix. We then apply the Eq. 1 to label the storage format that gives the smallest O for each training sample. Figure 6 lists the frequency of a storage format to be found to be optimal on our training dataset. Here, the x-axis shows different settings of w in Eq. 1. As can be seen from the diagram, the optimal storage format can vary depending on the optimization criterion. Our approach can adapt to such changes by automatically learning from the training samples (see Sect. 4.5).

For each training data sample, we also extract the values of a selected set of features (described in Sect. 4.4). We note that training is a one-off cost, and the trained predictive model can be used by any GNN model to optimize the SpMM computation kernel.

4.4   Feature Engineering

Feature Selection. A key aspect in building a good machine learning predictor is finding the right representation, or *features*, to capture the essential characteristics of the input workload. We start by considering over 30 raw features chosen based on previous work of SPMV optimization [27]. Most of the features

Table 2. Matrix feature used by in our predictive model

No.	Featur.	Description	No.	Featur.	Description
F1	numRow	# rows	F2	numCol	# columns
F3	NNZ	# Non-zeros	F4	N_diags	# diagonals
F5	aver_RD	Avg. # non-zero elements per row	F6	max_RD	Max. # non-zeros per row
F7	min_RD	Min. # non-zeros per row	F8	dev_RD	Standard deviation of non-zero numbers per row
F9	aver_CD	Avg. # non-zeros per column	F10	max_CD	Max. # non-zero values per column
F11	min_CD	Min. # non-zero values per column	F12	dev_CD	The deviation number of non-zeros per column
F13	ER_DIA	Ratio of non-zeros in diagonals	F14	ER_CD	Ratio of non-zeros in column-packed structure
F15	row_bounce	Avg. differences between non-zeros of adjacent rows	F16	col_bounce	Avg. difference between non-zeros of adjacent columns
F17	density	Density of non-zeros	F18	cv	Normalized variation of non-zeros per row
F19	max_mu	max. RD - avg. RD			

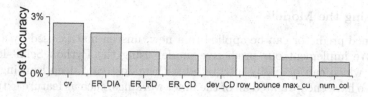

Fig. 7. Top-8 features which can lead to a high loss in accuracy if they are not used.

are used to capture the distribution of non-zero elements of the input matrix, which can be extracted in parallel to reduce the overhead of feature extraction.

To learn effectively over a small training dataset, we use the feature score given as a by-product of the XGBoost training process to select a compact set of features. The feature score is computed summing up how many times each feature is split on the decision tree. We then keep features that contribute to 95% of the aggregated importance scores across all raw features. Using a fewer number of features also help us to reduce the overhead of runtime feature extraction. Table 2 summarizes our chosen matrix features.

Feature Normalization. In the final step, we scale each of the extracted feature values to a common range (between 0 and 1) to prevent the range of any single feature from being a factor in its importance. We record the minimum and maximum values of each feature in the training dataset in order to scale the feature values of an unseen matrix. We also clip a feature value to make sure it is within the expected range during deployment.

Feature Importance. Figure 7 shows the top 8 dominant features based on their impact on our predictive model accuracy. We calculate feature importance by first training a model using all 19 of our chosen features, and record the accuracy of our model. In turn, we then remove each of our features, retraining and evaluating our model on the other 18, noting the drop in prediction accuracy. We then normalize the values to produce a percentage of importance for each of our features. Features for measuring the non-zero element distribution, like ER_DIA and cv in Table 2, are important for choosing the storage format. The similar distribution of feature importance is an indication that each of our features is able to represent distinct information about the matrix workload, all of which is important for the prediction task at hand.

4.5   Training the Model

The collected feature values, together with the desired label for each training matrix, are passed to a supervised learning algorithm to learn the XGBoost model. The time for training the predictor is dominated by generating the training data. In this work, it takes less than a week to label all the training samples using a single multi-core server. In comparison, processing the raw data and building the models took a negligible amount of time, less than an hour run in a RTX 2060 GPU. Since training is only performed once, it is a *one-off* cost.

4.6 Using the Model

The trained predictor can be applied to a new, unseen matrix used by a SpMM kernel. We implement our predictive model using the Python Scikit-learn [4] package, which can be easily integrated with mainstream deep learning frameworks. We have encapsulated all of the inner workings, such as feature extraction, prediction and storage format conversion and kernel selection, into a single package. Prediction is done by calling a dedicated SpMMPredict function (provided by our library) before each GNN layer. The function takes as input a matrix object and outputs a matrix object stored using the predicted storage format. Depending on the matrix object type, the corresponding SpMM kernel will be automatically chosen. Our current implementation supports PyTorch, but it can be easily ported to other deep learning frameworks.

5 Experimental Setup

5.1 Software and Hardware

Evaluation Platform. Our hardware platform is a dual-socket multi-core server with two 20-core Intel Sky Lake Xeon Gold 6138 CPUs running at 2.0 Ghz with 192 GB of RAM. Our evaluation platform runs Centos 7 with Linux kernel version 3.10. We test our approach on PyTorch v1.4.0, running on the CPU.

GNN Models. We apply our approach to 5 representative GNN architectures, including GCN, graph attention network (GAT) [30], relational graph convolutional neural network (RGCN) [26], GNN with feature-wise linear modulation (FiLM) [3] and efficient graph convolutions (EGN) [28]. We use the open-source implementation provided by PyTorch-geometric library [11] by stacking two GNN layers to form a standard graph model.

Datasets. In our evaluation, we use two graph data suites, CoraFull [40] and Entities [26], containing a total of 5 graph datasets with matrix sizes ranging from 19,793 to 58,086. To evaluate the generalization ability of our approach, we also apply our approach to 100 synthetic matrices of different sizes and sparsity. For the synthetic data, we initialize weights in the adjacency matrices by populating them with random single floating numbers between 0 and 1.0.

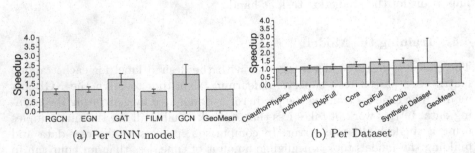

Fig. 8. Speedup given by our approach over COO. GeoMean represents the geometric mean given by the previous performance.

5.2   Evaluation Methodology

Competitive methods. We compare our approach against two closely related predictive methods for using machine learning to choose the sparse matrix storage format. The first approach employs a convolutional neural network (CNN) [24,45], and the second uses a decision tree model for format selection [27]. We use an open-source implementation of ResNet [23] as the CNN model. To provide a fair comparison, we train all machine learning models on the same training dataset using the methodology described in the source publications.

Performance Report. We consider the end-to-end execution time, including the overhead of our predictive model (i.e., the time spending on feature extraction, storage format transformation and model prediction). Our feature extraction process runs in parallel using all CPU cores. We measure the end-to-end training time by training each model on each dataset for 10 epochs. We run each matrix input 5 times and report the *geometric mean* of the end-to-end training time and show the variations across different runs as a min-max bar. Note that we only need to decide the matrix storage format once for each GNN layer across training epochs. Given that in our evaluation, the sparse matrix distribution is similar across training epochs, and hence the overhead of our approach can be further amortised across multiple training epochs.

6   Experimental Results

6.1   Overall Results

Figure 8(a) shows the speedup over the PyTorch COO sparse matrix storage format for each GNN model across our evaluation datasets. Here, the min-max bar show the variance across the evaluated datasets. In this experiment, we aim to optimize for speedups by setting w of Eq. 1. Moreover, in Sect. 6.4 we show our approach can generalize to other settings of w.

As can be seen from the diagrams, choosing the right sparse matrix storage format can improve the GNN performance. Our approach delivers an average speedup of 1.3x (up to 3x) on GCN, which involves many SpMM computations when performing the graph convolution operations. Our approach gives less performance improvement on RGCN because the dataset that RGCN operates is a dense edge-based dataset that does not benefit from sparse matrix format selection. Furthermore, on a small number of datasets, where the COO is the best format, our approach shows a minor slowdown, less than 7%, due to the overhead of feature extraction. But for the majority of the evaluated datasets, our approach gives a noticeable improvement over COO. Overall, our techniques give an average speedup of 1.17x across GNN models and evaluation datasets.

Figure 8(b) shows the achieved performance per real-world graph dataset across models. For most of the datasets, our approach gives noticeable speedups across GNN.

Table 3. Comparing our XGBoost approach with prior work

Model	Inference time (s)	Prediction accuracy (%)	Realized speedup
XGboost (ours)	0.0008	89.1	1.17
CNN [24,45]	0.002	66.8	0.86
Decision-Tree [27]	0.0002	83.8	1.14

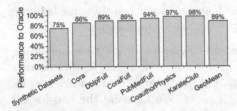

Fig. 9. Performance of our approach related to the Oracle performance.

Fig. 10. Prediction accuracy of our approach when varying w in Eq. 1.

6.2   Compare to Prior Methods

Table 3 compares our approach against a CNN and a decision tree model for choosing the matrix storage format, where our approach gives a better overall prediction accuracy. The CNN model gives a poor prediction accuracy when the model is trained on 300 synthetic matrices. While the performance of the CNN model can be improved by using more training data, doing so would incur a higher overhead. Table 3 confirms that a higher prediction accuracy does translate into better speedup performance, where our approach improves the CNN and the decision tree model by 27% and 3%, respectively.

6.3   Compare to Oracle Performance

Figure 9 compares our approach against *a theoretically perfect predictor* for storage form selection, for which we call *oracle*. We obtain the oracle performance by exhaustively profiling all candidate storage formats for each GNN layer to find out the best-performing format. The results show how close our predictive modeling approach is to the theoretical upper bound. Our approach achieves, on average, 89% of the oracle performance. Our model can be further improved by using more training samples together with more representative features to characterise some of the input matrices better to improve the prediction accuracy.

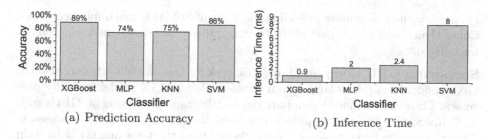

Fig. 11. Comparing our XGBoost model against alternative modeling techniques.

6.4   Model Analysis

Impact of optimization goal. Our evaluation so far set w to 1 of our optimization function (Eq. 1) by solely optimizing for speeds. Figure 10 shows prediction accuracy when we vary the parameter settings. Our approach has a good generalization by giving the average accuracy of 90%. This experiment shows that our approach is flexible and can adapt to different optimization trade-offs.

Alternative Modeling Techniques. Figure 11 compares our XGBoost-based predictor against three other classification methods used in prior works for code optimization [34]: MLP neural network [12], KNN (with $k = 1$) [42], and SVM [22]. All the alternative techniques were trained and evaluated using the same method and training data as our model. In this experiment, we consider the model prediction accuracy and the time for making a prediction. As can be seen from the diagram, our approach has the lowest runtime overhead while giving the highest accuracy when compared to alternative modeling techniques. Since XGBoost is a decision-tree-based model, it also has the advantage of being interpretable because its decision process can be followed by traversing the tree.

Training and Deployment Overhead. Training of our predictive model only needs to be performed once, after which the trained model can be applied to any matrices. Training is dominated by the generation of training data which takes in total less than a week's machine time (Sect. 4.3). We can speed this up by using multiple machines. The overhead for learning the XGBoost model is negligible, less than 5 min. Our approach has a negligible runtime overhead compared to the GNN kernel execution time, the overhead of feature extraction and prediction is less than 3% to the end-to-end kernel execution time.

6.5   Discussion

Supporting Other Storage Formats. Our approach can be easily extended to support other sparse matrix storage formats. As we formulate the storage format prediction as a classification problem, this can be achieved by adding a new class label (for the newly supported format) into our training dataset.

Doing so would also require providing the relevant SpMM kernel implementation. Other than these, a large part of the training process and deployment can remain unchanged.

Supporting GPU Computation. This work focuses on the CPU execution of GNN models due to the large graph datasets that a GNN model typically processes. There are methods to support large-scale graph processing on GPUs such as GraphSAGE [15]. Our approach can be ported to support GPU processing. This will require using training data collected from the targeting GPU to train our predictive model.

Optimize SpMM Algorithms. Optimizing SpMM computation is an active research field [10]. It is interesting to investigate how the SpMM computation kernel can be tailored for GNN computation and what parameters can be opened to a tuning framework. As the best algorithm parameters are likely to change depending on the matrix input and the underlying hardware, an automatic machine learning-based approach similar to our approach is highly attractive.

7   Related Work

Several approaches have been proposed to optimize graph processing [39]. Some provide new programming abstractions to optimize vertex/node-centric or edge-centric processing [46]. For example, Pytorch-Geometric (PyG) [11] and Deep Graph Library (DGL) [33] are two major frameworks for GNN computation. Both libraries rely on a low-level, hand-optimized SpMM library, but they use a single sparse matrix storage format throughout the execution. Our work complements these prior efforts by dynamically adapting the sparse matrix storage format and the associated computation kernel for each GNN layer, which can be easily integrated with existing graph programming models.

Various sparse matrix storage formats have been proposed in the past [19]. Studies have shown that there is no "one-fit-for-all" storage format, and the right format can change from one matrix to the other [6, 20]. Methods have been proposed to dynamically choose sparse matrix storage format based on the input workloads [27]. These include approaches build around analytical methods [31] or machine-learning-based predictive models [5]. The latter has the benefit of can be easily ported to different architectures as machine learning learns from empirical observations rather than simplified assumptions used by an analytical model. However, prior machine-learning-based solutions have been concentrated on optimizing sparse matrix-vector multiplication (SpMV) of scientific workloads [45]. They choose a storage format at the beginning of the program execution but do not adjust the format during application execution. No work so far has concerned choosing the sparse matrix storage format for GNN SpMM throughout program execution. Our work is the first to do so.

Machine learning is a proven design methodology for systems modeling and optimization [25, 34, 35, 38, 43, 44]. Studies have demonstrated the success of applying machine learning for a wide range of code optimization tasks

[9,29,32,36,37,41] In this work, we employ machine learning techniques to develop an automatic approach to optimize GNN SpMM. We remark that our work does not seek to advance machine learning algorithms; instead, it explores and applies a well-established modeling method to tackle the GNN SpMM optimization problem.

8   Conclusions

This paper has presented a machine-learning based predictive model to dynamically choose the sparse matrix storage format and the associate computation kernel during GNN execution. Our model uses numerical features to characterize the input matrix to predict the storage format to use for the next GNN layer. We evaluate our approach by applying it to five representative GNN models running on a multi-core CPU using both real-world and synthetic datasets. Experimental results show that our approach gives an average speedup of 1.17x (up to 3x) over the Pytorch default strategy and exhibits a good generalization ability.

References

1. Abadi, M., et al.: TensorFlow: a system for large-scale machine learning. In: OSDI (2016)
2. Bojchevski, A., Günnemann, S.: Deep gaussian embedding of graphs: unsupervised inductive learning via ranking. arXiv (2017)
3. Brockschmidt, M.: GNN-film: graph neural networks with feature-wise linear modulation. In: ICML 2020, 13–18 July 2020, Virtual Event (2020)
4. Buitinck, L., et al.: API design for machine learning software: experiences from the scikit-learn project. In: ECML PKDD Workshop (2013)
5. Chen, D., et al.: Optimizing sparse matrix-vector multiplications on an ARMv8-based many-core architecture. Int. J. Parallel Prog. **47**, 418–432 (2019)
6. Chen, D., et al.: Characterizing scalability of sparse matrix-vector multiplications on Phytium FT-2000+. Int. J. Parallel Prog. **1**, 80–97 (2020)
7. Chen, T., et al.: Xgboost: extreme gradient boosting. R Package **1**(4), 1–4 (2015)
8. Cui, P., et al.: A survey on network embedding. IEEE TKDE **31**(5), 833–852 (2018)
9. Cummins, C., et al.: End-to-end deep learning of optimization heuristics. In: PACT (2017)
10. Dalton, S., et al.: Optimizing sparse matrix-matrix multiplication for the GPU. ACM TOMS **41**, 1–20 (2015)
11. Fey, M., Lenssen, J.E.: Fast graph representation learning with pytorch geometric. arXiv (2019)
12. Gardner, M.W., Dorling, S.: Artificial neural networks (the multilayer perceptron)-a review of applications in the atmospheric sciences. Atmos. Environ. **32**, 2627–2636 (1998)
13. Gilbert, J.R., et al.: A unified framework for numerical and combinatorial computing. Comput. Sci. Eng. **10**(2), 20–25 (2008)
14. Greathouse, J.L., Daga, M.: Efficient sparse matrix-vector multiplication on GPUs using the CSR storage format. In: SC (2014)

15. Hamilton, W.L., et al.: Inductive representation learning on large graphs. In: NeurIPS (2017)
16. Hu, W., et al.: Open graph benchmark: Datasets for machine learning on graphs. arXiv (2020)
17. Huang, K., et al.: Understanding and bridging the gaps in current GNN performance optimizations. In: PPoPP (2021)
18. Kipf, T.N., Welling, M.: Semi-supervised classification with graph convolutional networks. arXiv (2016)
19. Langr, D., Tvrdik, P.: Evaluation criteria for sparse matrix storage formats. IEEE Trans. Parallel Distrib. Syst. **27**(2), 428–440 (2015)
20. Li, J., et al.: SMAT: an input adaptive auto-tuner for sparse matrix-vector multiplication. In: PLDI (2013)
21. Mehrabi, A., et al.: Learning sparse matrix row permutations for efficient SPMM on GPU architectures. In: ISPASS (2021)
22. Noble, W.S.: What is a support vector machine? Nat. Biotechnol. **24**, 1565–1567 (2006)
23. Paszke, A., et al.: Pytorch: An imperative style, high-performance deep learning library. In: Advances in Neural Information Processing Systems (2019)
24. Pichel, J.C., Pateiro-López, B.: Sparse matrix classification on imbalanced datasets using convolutional neural networks. IEEE Access (2019)
25. Ren, J., et al.: Optimise web browsing on heterogeneous mobile platforms: a machine learning based approach. In: INFOCOM (2017)
26. Schlichtkrull, M., Kipf, T.N., Bloem, P., van den Berg, R., Titov, I., Welling, M.: Modeling relational data with graph convolutional networks. In: Gangemi, A., et al. (eds.) ESWC 2018. LNCS, vol. 10843, pp. 593–607. Springer, Cham (2018). https://doi.org/10.1007/978-3-319-93417-4_38
27. Sedaghati, N., et al.: Automatic selection of sparse matrix representation on GPUs. In: ICS (2015)
28. Tailor, S.A., Opolka, F.L., Liò, P., Lane, N.D.: Adaptive filters and aggregator fusion for efficient graph convolutions (2021)
29. Tournavitis, G., et al.: Towards a holistic approach to auto-parallelization: integrating profile-driven parallelism detection and machine-learning based mapping. In: PLDI (2009)
30. Veličković, P., et al.: Graph attention networks (2018)
31. Venkat, A., et al.: Loop and data transformations for sparse matrix code. In: PLDI (2015)
32. Wang, H., et al.: Combining graph-based learning with automated data collection for code vulnerability detection. IEEE TIFS **16**, 1943–1958 (2020)
33. Wang, M., et al.: Deep graph library: towards efficient and scalable deep learning on graphs. (2019)
34. Wang, Z., O'Boyle, M.: Machine learning in compiler optimization. In: Proceedings of the IEEE (2018)
35. Wang, Z., O'Boyle, M.F.: Mapping parallelism to multi-cores: a machine learning based approach. In: PPoPP (2009)
36. Wang, Z., O'Boyle, M.F.: Partitioning streaming parallelism for multi-cores: a machine learning based approach. In: PACT (2010)
37. Wang, Z., et al.: Automatic and portable mapping of data parallel programs to OpenCL for GPU-based heterogeneous systems. ACM TACO **11**(4), 1–26 (2014)
38. Wang, Z., et al.: Integrating profile-driven parallelism detection and machine-learning-based mapping. ACM TACO **11**, 1–26 (2014)

39. Xie, Y., et al.: When do GNNs work: understanding and improving neighborhood aggregation. In: IJCAI (2020)
40. Xu, K., et al.: Cross-lingual knowledge graph alignment via graph matching neural network (2019)
41. Ye, G., et al.: Deep program structure modeling through multi-relational graph-based learning. In: PACT (2020)
42. Zhang, M.L., Zhou, Z.H.: ML-KNN: a lazy learning approach to multi-label learning. Pattern Recogn. **40**(7), 2038–2048 (2007)
43. Zhang, P., et al.: Auto-tuning streamed applications on Intel Xeon Phi. In: IPDPS (2018)
44. Zhang, P., et al.: Optimizing streaming parallelism on heterogeneous many-core architectures. IEEE TPDS **31**(8), 1878–1896 (2020)
45. Zhao, Y., et al.: Bridging the gap between deep learning and sparse matrix format selection. In: PPoPP (2018)
46. Zhou, J., et al.: Graph neural networks: a review of methods and applications. AI Open **1**, 57–81 (2020)

A Hybrid Synchronization Mechanism for Parallel Sparse Triangular Solve

Prabhjot Sandhu$^{(\boxtimes)}$, Clark Verbrugge, and Laurie Hendren

School of Computer Science, McGill University, Montreal, Canada
prabhjot.sandhu@mail.mcgill.ca, {clump,hendren}@cs.mcgill.ca

Abstract. Sparse triangular solve, SpTS, is an important and recurring component of many sparse linear solvers that are extensively used in many big-data analytics and machine learning algorithms. Despite its inherent sequential execution, a number of parallel algorithms like level-set and synchronization-free have been proposed. The coarse-grained synchronization mechanism of the level-set method uses a synchronization barrier between the generated level-sets, while the fine-grained synchronization approach of the sync-free algorithm makes use of atomic operations for each non-zero access. Both the synchronization mechanisms can prove to be expensive on CPUs for different sparsity structures of the matrices. We propose a novel and efficient synchronization approach which brings out the best of these two algorithms by avoiding the synchronization barrier while minimizing the use of atomic operations. Our web-based and parallel SpTS implementation with this hybrid synchronization mechanism, tested on around 2000 real-life sparse matrices, shows impressive performance speedups for a number of matrices over the classic level-set implementation.

Keywords: Sparse Matrix · Sparse Triangular Solve · SpTS · Performance · Level-set · Synchronization-free · WebAssembly

1 Introduction

While large and sparse matrices have historically been known to arise frequently in several scientific and compute-intensive applications, many modern big-data analytics and machine learning applications [2,10,12] have become their popular target these days. Likewise, the sparse matrix computations involved in these applications have also become critically important for their performance. Sparse triangular solve (SpTS) is one such recurring computation that is a building block of a number of sparse linear solver algorithms for sparse direct [5] and pre-conditioned iterative [19] methods in addition to the least-squares problems [3] which are widely used in the machine learning fields [15,24].

In this paper, we focus on SpTS which computes the solution vector x for the equation $Lx = y$, where L is a lower triangular sparse matrix, and y is a dense vector. It is a forward substitution algorithm where the solution of x_i may depend

© Springer Nature Switzerland AG 2022
X. Li and S. Chandrasekaran (Eds.): LCPC 2021, LNCS 13181, pp. 118–133, 2022.
https://doi.org/10.1007/978-3-030-99372-6_8

on the solution of $x_0,...,x_{i-1}$. The upper triangular case is analogous, and uses a backward substitution algorithm instead. Unlike other popular sparse kernels like sparse matrix-vector multiplication (SpMV), it is not straightforward to run SpTS operation in parallel, and achieve scalable performance due to this inherent sequential nature of the algorithm.

However, it is still possible to parallelize SpTS by exploiting the very nature of the sparse matrix. One way is to construct a dependency graph representing the dependencies between the components of the solution vector x, and then allow the independent ones to run in parallel. The popular *level-set* method for CPUs employs this approach to create the sets of independent components, and uses a coarse-grained synchronization method to maintain the dependency between those sets. Another algorithm called *synchronization-free* or *sync-free* for short, primarily used for GPUs, avoids generating the dependency information, and uses a fine-grained synchronization method to maintain the dependency between the components themselves. The *level-set* method uses barrier synchronization, while the *sync-free* method uses atomic operations.

Despite their differences, the effectiveness of both of these approaches depends on the sparsity structure of the matrix, and the machine architecture. It is highly impractical to use the *sync-free* method for CPUs due to the heavy use of expensive atomic operations on the limited number of threads over the entirety of this algorithm. A number of sparsity structure patterns can degrade the SpTS performance for the *level-set* method: (1) *large number of sets*, a sparsity structure with a large number of sets may hurt the SpTS performance due to the increased number of synchronization barriers; (2) *small and varied number of components per set*, a structure pattern with a few and a varying number of components per set may waste the assigned CPU resources and incur an unnecessary maintenance overhead; (3) *uneven distribution of non-zeros among the rows*, a sparsity structure with a highly uneven number of non-zeros to be processed for the components within the same set may lead to load imbalance among the worker threads. In order to address these challenges, we propose a synchronization mechanism that is less coarse-grained than the *level-set* method and less fine-grained than the *synchronization-free* method at the same time.

Following are the main contributions of our work in this paper:

- We present a novel synchronization approach, a hybrid between the *level-set* and *sync-free* algorithms, to efficiently run SpTS in parallel on CPUs. Our cost-effective busy-waiting synchronization strategy is built upon the use of two different synchronization modes and the dynamic switching between them.
- We employ a row classification technique to minimize the use of expensive atomic operations in the WebAssembly [8] environment.
- We tackle the issues with costly synchronization barriers between the level-sets by eliminating them, and developing SpTS to be less sensitive to the number of worker threads employed in comparison to the *level-set* method.
- We implement web-based and parallel SpTS using our hybrid synchronization method on WebAssembly and JavaScript, and evaluate its performance in comparison to the *level-set* method over almost 2000 real-life sparse matrices, and demonstrate impressive performance speedups.

2   Motivation and Related Work

SpTS, for being a key component of popular sparse linear solvers, continues to attract the attention of high-performance computing (HPC) researchers. The level-set method, proposed by Anderson and Saad [1] and Saltz [20] in the early 1990s, is a classic and well-known technique to solve SpTS in a parallel environment on CPUs. This graph-based algorithm involves a preprocessing step to create the level sets, and a costly synchronization barrier after each level to satisfy the dependencies between the levels. As a result, a number of recent research contributions have been made to analyze and overcome these limitations [18,25] and also to improve the parallel performance of this sparse kernel on modern machines [6,7,11,13,16,23].

Wolf et al. [25] analyzed a few factors like barrier type that impact the performance of multithreaded SpTS, favouring the use of more active barriers (spin locks) instead of the passive barriers (blocking locks). In order to reduce the performance overhead of inter-level synchronization, Park et al. [18] presented a synchronization sparsification technique that performs point-to-point synchronization between the *super tasks*, however with an involved and expensive preprocessing stage to reduce the number of dependency edges in the task dependency graph. While sharing the same goal, our synchronization strategy avoids both the synchronization barriers and the intricate preprocessing on the task dependency graph.

On the other hand, for manycore platforms, such as GPUs, Liu et al. [11] exposed the parallelism in SpTS for CSC storage format by making use of atomic operations for synchronization rather than creating the level-sets [6,16]. It is called a synchronization-free algorithm which reduced the preprocessing cost and completely eliminated the conventional synchronization between the levels. Dufrechou and Ezzati [7] later showed the performance improvements for sync-free algorithm using CSR format over the CSC format. Following this, Su et al. [23] recently proposed CapelliniSpTRSV, a thread-level instead of warp-level sync-free parallelism technique to improve the performance of matrices with a large number of rows per level and a small number of non-zeros per row. Lu et al. [13] implemented a recursive block algorithm to solve SpTS in parallel on GPUs while improving upon the two-dimensional blocking technique previously proposed by Mayer [14] to divide the triangular matrix into multiple triangular sub-matrices and rectangular or square sub-matrices.

Next, Yilmaz et al. [26] presented adaptive level binning to balance the workloads among the threads while making use of some features from both level-set and sync-free methods. Our approach in this paper is to reap the benefits of both level-set and sync-free methods in a more simplified and distinct manner to build an efficient sparse triangular solve. Several web-based machine learning frameworks like TensorFlow.js [17] train and deploy models in web browsers. Existing studies [9,21,22] have thus analyzed the performance of their extensively used sparse computations like SpMV in a web context. We develop a web-based sparse triangular solve which is also one of the most critical sparse BLAS (Basic Linear Algebra Subprograms) routines. In addition to that, our

```
for  i = 0 to N-1 do
  x[i] = 0
  for  j = row-ptr[i] to row-ptr[i+1] - 2 do
    x[i] += val[j] * x[col[j]]
  end for
  x[i] = (y[i] - x[i])/val[row-ptr[i+1] - 1]
end for
```

Listing 1.1. A serial SpTS CSR algorithm to solve x in Lx = y

work is a step towards building a web-based scientific computing framework that will provide optimized and parallel sparse BLAS routines, and has clear applicability as a high-performance backend for the leading ML frameworks.

3 Preliminaries

In this section, we provide some background details for SpTS operation which includes its widely used, classic and state-of-the-art serial and parallel algorithms.

3.1 Sparse Matrix and Serial SpTS

Given a nonsingular lower triangular sparse matrix in the external format, it is stored in the compressed sparse row (CSR) format as shown in Fig. 1. It is the most widely used internal sparse storage format which consists of three arrays row_ptr, col and val. While col and val arrays store the column index and the value of each non-zero entry in a row-major order, row_ptr array stores the starting index of each row, pointing at the other two arrays.

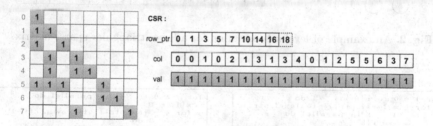

Fig. 1. An example of a lower triangular matrix in the CSR format.

In the serial SpTS CSR algorithm to solve x in the equation $Lx = y$, the sparse matrix rows are traversed sequentially, and each value of the solution vector x is solved accordingly. It is natural to solve it in this way because the solution of x_i may depend on the solution of $x_0,...,x_{i-1}$. As illustrated in Listing 1.1, for each x_i, the sum of the product of non-zero entries (excluding the diagonal entry) from the sparse matrix row i with the corresponding solutions of x, indicated via the column index of each non-zero entry, is calculated. Next, the solution of x_i is calculated by subtracting this sum from y_i, and then dividing it with the diagonal entry.

3.2 Parallel SpTS

Due to the sparse structure of a lower triangular sparse matrix in a SpTS operation, it is possible to find such matrix rows which are independent of each other, and can be solved in parallel. The level-set method and the synchronization-free algorithm are two popular techniques that exploit this property to run SpTS in parallel.

Level-Set. The preprocessing stage of this method makes sets of the matrix rows which can be solved independently and simultaneously as shown in Fig. 2 for the example matrix from Fig. 1. The cardinality of these sets describes the amount of parallelism available. A specific order is maintained between these sets, also called levels, to satisfy the dependency between them. This process basically converts the fine-grained dependencies between the rows into a coarse-grained dependency between the levels. In the parallel SpTS CSR level-set algorithm as shown in Listing 1.2, this coarse-grained dependency between the levels is satisfied by the use of a synchronization barrier after the completion of SpTS computation at each level.

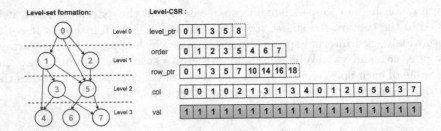

Fig. 2. An example of level-set formation for a lower triangular sparse matrix.

```
for l = 0 to nlevels - 1 do
  for k = level_ptr[l] to level_ptr[l
      +1] - 1 in parallel do
    i = order[k]
    x[i] = 0
    for j = row_ptr[i] to row_ptr[i
        +1] - 2 do
      x[i] += val[j] * x[col[j]]
    end for
    x[i] = (y[i] - x[i])/val[row_ptr[
        i+1] - 1]
  end for
  // barrier synchronization
end for
```

Listing 1.2. A simplified SpTS CSR level-set algorithm to solve x in Lx = y

```
for i = 0 to N-1 in parallel do
  x[i] = 0
  for j = row_ptr[i] to row_ptr[i+1]
      - 2 do
    while atomic_read(flag[col[j]])
        != 1 do
      // busy-wait
    end while
    x[i] += val[j] * x[col[j]]
  end for
  x[i] = (y[i] - x[i])/val[row_ptr[i
      +1] - 1]
  atomic_write(flag[i], 1)
end for
```

Listing 1.3. A simplified SpTS CSR sync-free algorithm to solve x in Lx = y

Synchronization-Free. This algorithm eliminates the cost of barrier synchronizations between the levels by establishing a busy-waiting mechanism and making use of expensive atomic load/store operations as shown in Listing 1.3.

4 Our Approach

In this section, we first give an overview of our approach, and next provide the details on the internals of our hybrid synchronization strategy.

4.1 Overview

The level-set method employs a coarse-grained synchronization mechanism that works at each level, while the sync-free method applies a fine-grained synchronization scheme that works at each row. Both of these synchronization mechanisms have their own benefits depending on the structure of the matrix. Theoretically, the sparse matrices with a few levels and a significant and balanced workload among the given worker threads will prefer the level-set method. The sync-free method may prove useful otherwise. However, the situation may be different at different levels depending on the structure of the matrix. Hence, we intend to follow a middle path between these two algorithms to reap the benefits of both. The objective of our algorithm is to improve the performance of parallel SpTS by avoiding the synchronization barrier while minimizing the use of atomic operations as much as possible.

(1) **No Synchronization Barrier with Level-Set Formation.** Unlike the sync-free approach, we choose to keep the preprocessing step of the level-set method. We build the level-set formation in a simplified manner, and reorder the rows to bring together the rows from the same level-set to have spatial locality. We adopt this formation because it is a systematic way to guarantee that the worker threads at the same level can make progress independently and simultaneously. This becomes the basis of our simplified synchronization technique.

However, like the sync-free algorithm, we decide to employ no barrier synchronization after each level because the worker thread does no useful work while waiting at the barrier. Instead, we allow each worker thread to immediately start processing the next level after it is done with the current level, without waiting for other worker threads to reach the end of the same level. In order to maintain the accuracy of the algorithm, we employ a novel and effective busy-waiting synchronization mechanism described in detail in the following sections.

(2) **Minimize the Use of Atomic Operations.** In the sync-free system as shown in Listing 1.3, an atomic load operation is performed repeatedly for each non-zero until the value of vector x at the *required row* (represented by the column index of the non-zero) is completely solved and available for use. This availability is indicated after the complete computation of the value of vector x at each row by using an atomic store operation. Due to the heavy use of expensive atomic operations on the limited number of threads over the entirety of this algorithm, this system proves highly ineffective on the CPUs.

However, in order to avoid the synchronization barrier, we need another synchronization strategy to make sure that the value of solution vector x at a given row is completely solved before its use. As a result, it seems appealing to develop a hybrid synchronization mechanism that brings out the best of both the level-set method and the sync-free method for CPUs. A straightforward candidate solution is to employ the sync-free busy-waiting mechanism for the worker threads which have been advanced to the next levels, while other worker threads are still working at the current level. However, it continues to be an unproductive solution as it still requires an atomic store operation for each row to indicate the availability of the value of solution vector x at a given row.

Therefore, we employ a number of techniques to minimize the use of atomic operations, and build a more cost-effective busy-waiting synchronization strategy. In addition to that, we also keep a simplified synchronization mechanism where no atomic operations and busy-waiting are needed. We call our two synchronization techniques as `no-busy-wait` and `busy-wait`, as shown in Fig. 3, and dynamically switch between the two during the course of SpTS computation as many times as required.

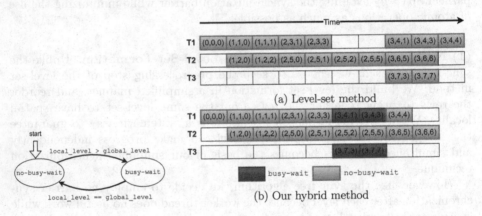

Fig. 3. Our synchronization modes and their dynamic switching conditions.

Fig. 4. An example with a timeline to show the parallel SpTS workflow for algorithms with different synchronization mechanisms.

4.2   no-busy-wait

This synchronization mode is set by default at the start of the SpTS computation. As the name implies, it doesn't involve any busy-waiting, and each thread can safely assume that the value of vector x at the *required row* is completely solved and available for use. Let's suppose `local_level` to be the current working level of a worker thread, and `global_level` to be the maximum working level achieved by all the worker threads. The value of `global_level` will always be less than or equal to `local_level` for any worker thread. A worker thread can work in this synchronization mode if its `local_level` is equal to `global_level`.

Otherwise, the worker thread continues its work for the next level after switching its synchronization mode to `busy-wait`, the details of which will be presented in the following section.

Let's use the example matrix and its level-set formation from Figs. 1 and 2 to inspect the SpTS workflow in a parallel environment while applying our synchronization strategy. We assume three worker threads T1, T2 and T3 in Fig. 4 to show the SpTS computation timeline with each 3-tuple representing (`local_level`, `row`, `column`) for the processing of each non-zero.

While processing the non-zero, the *required row* index for the vector x is represented by the `column` value of the 3-tuple. For example, the tuple (3,4,3) for the worker thread T1 means that the current working level of thread T1 is 3, and it is processing the non-zero at 4th row and 3rd column of the matrix, and it requires the value of $x[3]$ to proceed with the computation. All the worker threads start their work in the `no-busy-wait` mode as illustrated in Fig. 4b. The worker threads T1 and T3 switch to `busy-wait` as their `local_level` reaches 3, represented by the tuples (3,4,1) and (3,7,3) respectively. But at the same time, T2 continues to work in the `no-busy-wait` mode, keeping the value of `global_level` to be 2. If it had been the conventional level-set method as shown in Fig. 4a, the worker threads T1 and T3 must wait at the barrier until `global_level` becomes equal to their `local_level`, which happens after T2 also finishes its work at level 2.

4.3 busy-wait

A worker thread switches to this mode when its `local_level` becomes greater than `global_level` to allow itself to make feasible advancements and avoid the costly barrier. Unlike `no-busy-wait`, this mode doesn't provide any safety guarantees by default that the value of vector x at the *required row* is completely solved and available for use. As indicated earlier, the busy-waiting mechanism of the sync-free algorithm is a candidate solution, but it will require the worker thread to perform atomic store operations for each row even during the `no-busy-wait` mode. Therefore, we employed more cost-effective busy-waiting techniques to enable the worker thread to make progress in a safely manner.

We classify the required rows into four exhaustive categories: (1) *previous-level rows* (2) *intra-thread rows* (3) *advanced-worker inter-thread rows* (4) *inter-thread rows*. The worker thread identifies the *required row* to be one of these categories, and decides whether to proceed with the computation or wait. If the *required row* belongs to any one of them except (4), it is safe for the worker thread to perform the computation as illustrated by a flowchart in Fig. 5. It is due to this classification that we are able to minimize the use of atomic operations. Listing 1.4 shows a portion of SpTS implementation in WebAssembly, providing details of the internals of our technique in the `busy-wait` synchronization mode.

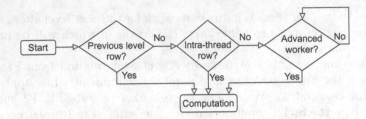

Fig. 5. An overview of the internals of the `busy-wait` synchronization mode for each non-zero in SpTS computation.

```
(f32.load (local.get $csr_val))
(i32.load (local.get $csr_col))
(local.set $required_row)
(i32.atomic.load (local.get $global_row_index))
(local.get $required_row)
(i32.le_s)
if
  (i32.load (i32.add (local.get $row_worker_index) (i32.shl (local.get
      $required_row) (i32.const 2))))
  (local.set $worker)
  (local.get $worker)
  (local.get $current_worker)
  (i32.ne)
  if
    (i32.load (i32.add (local.get $row_level_index) (i32.shl (local.get
        $required_row) (i32.const 2))))
    (local.set $required_level)
    (loop $busy_wait_loop
      (local.get $required_level)
      (i32.atomic.load (i32.add (local.get $worker_level_index) (i32.shl (
          local.get $worker) (i32.const 2))))
      (i32.gt_s)
      (br_if $busy_wait_loop)
    )
  end
end
(f32.load (i32.add (local.get $x) (i32.shl (local.get $required_row) (i32.const 2)
  ))) (f32.mul)
```

Listing 1.4. A portion of SpTS WebAssembly implementation in the `busy-wait` synchronization mode

(1) Previous Level Rows are the rows that belong to the preceding levels which have been completed by all the worker threads. It means the value of x at the required rows from this category must be available for use. We use `global_row_index` to represent the maximum row index of the level completed by all the worker threads. This value is atomically updated to the maximum row index of a particular level when all the worker threads finish their computation at that level. The worker thread atomically reads this value to identify the category of its required row. If `global_row_index` is greater than the required row, it is confirmed that the required row belongs to this category.

For example, the worker thread T1 from Fig. 4b in the `busy-wait` mode at the tuple (3,4,1) identifies that the required row 1 (represented by the column value of this tuple) belongs to the previous level category, and hence proceeds with the computation.

(2) Intra-thread Rows are the rows processed by the worker thread itself. It means the value of x at those required rows must already be completely solved.

We statically store the mapping between the rows and the worker threads. The worker thread uses this information to identify if the required row belongs to this category. Since this mapping is static, non-atomic loads are sufficient to perform this check.

For example, in the `busy-wait` mode, the required row 3 from the tuple (3,4,3) of the worker thread T1 in Fig. 4b was indeed processed by T1 itself. Therefore, it qualifies as an intra-thread row, and T1 goes on to carry out the computation.

(3) Advanced-Worker Inter-thread Rows are the rows that are processed by other worker threads which are also ahead of `global_level`. In addition to that, these rows belong to those levels which are already completed by those worker threads. We statically have the mapping between the rows and the level sets, and also between the rows and the worker threads. The required level and the corresponding worker thread information is calculated using these mappings. Each worker thread atomically updates its recently completed level as it proceeds with its computations. Therefore, the given worker thread atomically reads the recently completed level of the corresponding worker thread. If it is greater than or equal to the required level, the given worker thread can safely assume that the value of x at the required row is available for use.

For example, the required row 3 belongs to the advanced-worker inter-thread category for worker thread T3 at the tuple (3,7,3) in Fig. 4b. T3 determines this by checking that the required row 3 and its corresponding level 2 have been completely processed by the advanced worker thread T1.

(4) Inter-thread Rows are the rows that are processed by other worker threads, and belong to the level which is not yet finished by those worker threads. Hence, the given worker thread needs to wait for the value to become available. In contrast to the sync-free algorithm, each worker thread atomically declares the completion of a level instead of the completion of a row as it proceeds with its computations. We have followed this style to reduce the cost of atomic store operations.

Since this mode involves busy-waiting, it is naturally more expensive than the `no-busy-wait` mode. In order to keep the benefits of not performing the atomic load operations when not needed, a worker thread checks before the computation on each non-zero if it is possible to switch back to its default synchronization mode. Therefore, the worker thread switches back to `no-busy-wait` mode if its `local_level` becomes equal to `global_level`.

5 Evaluation

In this section, we first describe our experimental layout. Next, we evaluate the SpTS performance using our WebAssembly implementations of both hybrid and level-set synchronization methods on our benchmark matrices.

5.1   Experimental Setup

We conducted our experiments on an Intel Core i7-3930K with 6 3.20 GHz cores, 12 MB last-level cache and 16 GB memory, running Ubuntu Linux 18.04.5. Our execution environment for WebAssembly is the Chrome 92 browser (Official build 92.0.4515.107 with V8 JavaScript engine 9.2.230.20). We ran headless Chrome with two flags, `--wasm-no-bounds-checks` and `--wasm-no-stack-checks` to avoid memory bounds checks and stack guards for performance testing. We used `Date.now()`, a JavaScript method to measure the execution time.

Our set of sparse matrix benchmarks consists of 1,957 real-life square sparse matrices from The SuiteSparse Matrix Collection [4]. We use Matrix Market external format as an input to our programs, and store the lower triangular portion of the sparse matrices in the internal format to solve Lx = y. We keep all the diagonal elements to be non-zeros to avoid the sparse matrix from being singular.

5.2   SpTS Performance Comparison

Figure 6 shows the single-precision SpTS performance speedup of using hybrid over level-set synchronization method for our benchmark matrices with *CSR Working Set* on the x-axis, which is calculated as $((nlevels + 1) + (N + 1) + 2 * nnz + 2 * N) * 4$, where *nlevels* is the number of generated levels for a $N X N$ lower triangular sparse matrix with *nnz* number of non-zeros.

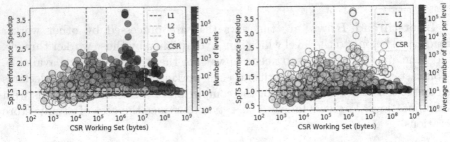

(a) Speedup vs number of levels   (b) Speedup vs avg number of rows per level

Fig. 6. Performance speedup of our hybrid method over the level-set method for different sparse matrices depicted using different structure features

It is evident that the hybrid method shows quite promising performance speedups for a number of matrices especially with a large number of levels. Apart from that, we notice various different speedup results for different sparse matrices from the plot. It indicates that the choice of synchronization method can have a significant impact on the SpTS performance. Using our observation, we classify the speedup results into three categories: (1) *Below 1* (2) *Above 1* (3) *Close to 1*, and evaluate them on an individual basis.

Below 1. This category belongs to the set of matrices that shows better SpTS performance for the level-set synchronization method. Figure 6 clearly shows that the *CSR Working Set* size of the matrices from this category is usually small. In order to understand the properties of this set, we show a small subset of these matrices in Table 1, which largely represents the whole set of the *Below 1* matrices. First of all, we can observe from this table that some of these matrices have a large number of rows per level. It indicates that each worker thread likely receives a substantial amount of workload. Further examination uncovers that there is a nearly balanced workload among the worker threads at each level for these matrices. Since the cost of synchronization barriers becomes insignificant due to the nearly balanced and significant workload, these matrices perform better with the level-set synchronization method.

Table 1. Representative matrices from Below 1 category

Matrix	N	nnz	nlevels	N/nlevels	Performance(GFLOPS)		Speedup
					Level-set	Hybrid	
t2dal_e	4257	4257	1	4257	1.70	1.52	0.89x
iprob	3001	6001	2	1500.5	2.96	2.71	0.92x
bcsstm11	1473	1473	1	1473	1.37	1.07	0.78x
grid2	3296	9728	3	1098.6	3.36	3.07	0.91x
SmaGri	1059	1117	4	264.7	0.59	0.46	0.78x
fpga_dcop_09	1220	3857	6	203.3	1.49	1.34	0.89x
bcspwr08	1624	3837	14	116	0.89	0.74	0.83x
t3dl_a	20360	265113	633	32.2	1.32	1.22	0.92x
exdata_1	6001	1137751	1501	3.99	1.47	1.37	0.93x
psmigr_3	3140	278874	1638	1.91	0.89	0.82	0.92x

Next, the matrices with a very small number of rows per level like *psmigr_3* indicate that almost no parallelism is available for the worker threads. However, the large number of non-zeros per row likely reduces the cost of synchronization barriers. Therefore, in both of these conditions, our approach suffers from the overhead of switching the synchronization modes via function calls and the atomic operations performed.

Above 1. This set of matrices shows better SpTS performance for the hybrid synchronization method. We list the details and the actual performance numbers of a small subset of these matrices in Table 2. First of all, we can observe from this table that these matrices have a large number of levels which means there are a large number of synchronization barriers involved for the level-set method.

Next, there are a small to moderate number of rows per level which indicates that a limited amount of workload is available for each worker thread. Our further investigation reveals that the distribution of rows among the levels is highly uneven. A small number of levels have a very large number of rows,

Table 2. Representative matrices from Above 1 category

Matrix	N	nnz	nlevels	N/nlevels	Performance(GFLOPS)		Speedup
					Level-set	Hybrid	
lung2	109460	273647	479	228.5	1.47	2.28	1.55x
dblp-2010	326186	1133886	1562	208.8	1.43	1.8	1.25x
delaunay_n17	131072	524248	910	144.0	1.36	1.82	1.34x
shallow_water1	81920	204800	1016	80.6	0.58	0.87	1.50x
twotone	120750	734744	1695	71.2	1.28	1.72	1.34x
e40r0100	17281	257727	512	33.7	1.49	2.06	1.38x
ted_A	10605	313099	1217	8.7	1.10	1.74	1.58x
ship_001	34920	1965708	4654	7.5	1.33	1.66	1.25x
smt	25710	1887646	4646	5.5	1.27	1.72	1.35x
t2em	921632	2756232	871133	1.05	0.012	0.028	2.33x

while others have quite small. This imbalanced distribution of rows among the levels further limits the amount of workload per worker thread, leading them to be stuck at the synchronization barrier most of their lifetime for the level-set method. On the other hand, our approach benefits from allowing the worker threads to move to further levels to perform some feasible part of the SpTS computation.

Finally, there are a few matrices like *t2em* with a large number of levels and a very small number of rows per level. Although these matrices show great performance speedup for the hybrid method, they are potentially less interesting for the comparison due to their nearly nonexistent parallelism, and low absolute performance numbers.

Close to 1. Finally, this set of matrices shows similar SpTS performance for both hybrid and level-set synchronization methods. We show a small subset of these matrices along with their structure parameters in Table 3.

It is intriguing to notice that the matrices from this category have a varied number of levels, starting from as low as 1 and ranging up to a large number. We observe the presence of diagonal matrices of different sizes (with a number of levels equal to 1) in both *Below 1* and *Close to 1* categories. It shows that the overhead becomes insignificant for the large matrices with a small number of levels. However, for the matrices with a large number of levels, we investigated to find out that the workload among the worker threads at each level is a little imbalanced. The workload imbalance is such that the SpTS performance gain from some levels in our approach gets cancelled out by the overhead from other levels.

Table 3. Representative matrices from Close to 1 category

Matrix	N	nnz	nlevels	N/nlevels	Performance(GFLOPS)		Speedup
					Level-set	Hybrid	
mbeacxc	496	30309	214	2.3	0.76	0.76	1.00x
s3dkq4m2	90449	2259087	2369	38.2	1.39	1.40	1.01x
coPapersCiteseer	434102	16470822	8087	53.7	2.26	2.24	0.99x
TSOPF_RS_b39_c7	14098	238270	106	133	3.20	3.22	1.01x
kron_g500-logn18	262144	10844830	1820	144	1.21	1.19	0.98x
wikipedia-20051105	1634989	15512976	1273	1284.3	1.68	1.68	1.00x
hangGlider_5	16011	89187	6	2668.5	3.97	4.03	1.02x
t3dl_e	20360	20360	1	20360	1.87	1.83	0.98x
rajat29	643994	2294300	29	22206.6	3.97	4.03	1.01x
ins2	309412	1530448	8	38676.5	3.11	3.14	1.01x
parabolic_fem	525825	2100225	7	75117.8	4.27	4.27	1.00x

The analysis of these three different types of speedup results demonstrates the impact of the structure of the matrix on the choice of the synchronization method. A single synchronization method is therefore not appropriate for all the given input matrices. Our evaluations prove the potential of our hybrid method to support an adaptive synchronization technique for SpTS on CPUs based on the structure of the matrix.

6   Conclusion and Future Work

The limitations of the level-set method for different sparsity structures of the matrices, and the ineffectiveness of the sync-free algorithm on CPUs led us to develop our hybrid synchronization method. Our strategy specifically targeted the granularity of the existing synchronization techniques to overcome their performance bottlenecks. While keeping the level-set formation, we avoided the synchronization barriers and minimized the use of atomic operations. We tested our WebAssembly SpTS implementation with this hybrid synchronization approach on around 2000 matrices, and demonstrated impressive speedups for several matrices over the classic level-set implementation.

Our future directions include the exploration of more sparse storage formats and optimization techniques like SIMD in addition to the improvements over the present parallelization strategies. It involves using the upcoming synchronization constructs like atomic floating-point operations from the rapidly expanding WebAssembly instruction set. Besides, the non-trivial task to automatically figure out the best synchronization method for SpTS at runtime for a given sparse matrix has intrigued us to explore the pertinent matrix structure features for developing such techniques in the future.

Acknowledgments. This work was supported by the COHESA project, through NSERC Strategic Networks grant NETGP485577-15.

References

1. Anderson, E., Saad, Y.: Solving sparse triangular linear systems on parallel computers. Int. J. High Speed Comput. **1**(1), 73–95 (1989)
2. Liu, B., Wang, M., Foroosh, H., Tappen, M., Penksy, M.: Sparse convolutional neural networks. In: 2015 IEEE Conference on Computer Vision and Pattern Recognition (CVPR), pp. 806–814 (2015)
3. Björck, A.: Numerical Methods for Least Squares Problems. Society for Industrial and Applied Mathematics (1996)
4. Davis, T.A., Hu, Y.: The University of Florida sparse matrix collection. ACM Trans. Math. Softw. (TOMS) **38**(1), 1 (2011)
5. Duff, I.S., Erisman, A.M., Reid, J.K.: Direct Methods for Sparse Matrices. Oxford University Press Inc, Oxford (1986)
6. Dufrechou, E., Ezzatti, P.: A new GPU algorithm to compute a level set-based analysis for the parallel solution of sparse triangular systems. In: IEEE International Parallel and Distributed Processing Symposium (IPDPS), pp. 920–929 (2018)
7. Dufrechou, E., Ezzatti, P.: Solving sparse triangular linear systems in modern GPUs: a synchronization-free algorithm. In: 26th Euromicro International Conference on Parallel, Distributed and Network-Based Processing (PDP), pp. 196–203 (2018)
8. Haas, A., et al.: Bringing the web up to speed with web assembly. In: PLDI 2017, pp. 185–200. ACM (2017)
9. Herrera, D., Chen, H., Lavoie, E., Hendren, L.: Numerical computing on the web: Benchmarking for the future. In: Proceedings of the 14th ACM SIGPLAN International Symposium on Dynamic Languages, pp. 88–100. DLS 2018. ACM, New York, NY, USA (2018)
10. Kepner, J., Gilbert, J.: Graph Algorithms in the Language of Linear Algebra. Society for Industrial and Applied Mathematics (2011)
11. Liu, W., Li, A., Hogg, J., Duff, I.S., Vinter, B.: A synchronization-free algorithm for parallel sparse triangular solves. In: Dutot, P.-F., Trystram, D. (eds.) Euro-Par 2016. LNCS, vol. 9833, pp. 617–630. Springer, Cham (2016). https://doi.org/10.1007/978-3-319-43659-3_45
12. Low, Y., Gonzalez, J., Kyrola, A., Bickson, D., Guestrin, C., Hellerstein, J.: GraphLab: a new framework for parallel machine learning. In: Proceedings of the Twenty-Sixth Conference on Uncertainty in Artificial Intelligence, pp. 340–349, UAI 2010. AUAI Press, Arlington, Virginia, USA (2010)
13. Lu, Z., Niu, Y., Liu, W.: Efficient block algorithms for parallel sparse triangular solve. In: 49th International Conference on Parallel Processing - ICPP, ICPP 2020. Association for Computing Machinery, New York, NY, USA (2020)
14. Mayer, J.: Parallel algorithms for solving linear systems with sparse triangular matrices. Computing **86**(4), 291–312 (2009)
15. Natarajan, R., Sindhwani, V., Tatikonda, S.: Sparse least-squares methods in the parallel machine learning (PML) framework. In: 2009 IEEE International Conference on Data Mining Workshops, pp. 314–319 (2009)
16. Naumov, M.: Parallel solution of sparse triangular linear systems in the preconditioned iterative methods on the GPU. NVIDIA Corp., Westford, MA, USA, Technical report, NVR-2011 (2011)
17. Thorat, N., Smilkov, D., Nicholson, C.: TensorFlow.js - a WebGL accelerated browser based JavaScript library for training and deploying ML models. https://js.tensorflow.org

18. Park, J., Smelyanskiy, M., Sundaram, N., Dubey, P.: Sparsifying synchronization for high-performance shared-memory sparse triangular solver. In: Kunkel, J.M., Ludwig, T., Meuer, H.W. (eds.) ISC 2014. LNCS, vol. 8488, pp. 124–140. Springer, Cham (2014). https://doi.org/10.1007/978-3-319-07518-1_8
19. Saad, Y.: Iterative Methods for Sparse Linear Systems. Society for Industrial and Applied Mathematics (2003)
20. Saltz, J.H.: Aggregation methods for solving sparse triangular systems on multi-processors. SIAM J. Sci. Stat. Comput. 11(1), 123–144 (1990)
21. Sandhu, P., Herrera, D., Hendren, L.: Sparse matrices on the web: characterizing the performance and optimal format selection of sparse matrix-vector multiplication in Javascript and Webassembly. In: Proceedings of the 15th International Conference on Managed Languages & Runtimes. ManLang 2018. Association for Computing Machinery, New York, NY, USA (2018)
22. Sandhu, P., Verbrugge, C., Hendren, L.: A fully structure-driven performance analysis of sparse matrix-vector multiplication. In: Proceedings of the ACM/SPEC International Conference on Performance Engineering, pp. 108–119, ICPE 2020. Association for Computing Machinery, New York, NY, USA (2020)
23. Su, J., et al.: CapelliniSpTRSV: a thread-level synchronization-free sparse triangular solve on GPUs. In: 49th International Conference on Parallel Processing - ICPP, ICPP 2020. Association for Computing Machinery, New York, NY, USA (2020)
24. Sun, L., Ji, S., Ye, J.: A least squares formulation for a class of generalized eigenvalue problems in machine learning. In: Proceedings of the 26th Annual International Conference on Machine Learning, pp. 977–984, ICML 2009. Association for Computing Machinery, New York, NY, USA (2009)
25. Wolf, M.M., Heroux, M.A., Boman, E.G.: Factors impacting performance of multithreaded sparse triangular solve. In: Palma, J.M.L.M., Daydé, M., Marques, O., Lopes, J.C. (eds.) High Performance Computing for Computational Science - VECPAR 2010, pp. 32–44. Springer, Heidelberg (2011). https://doi.org/10.1007/978-3-642-19328-6_6
26. Yılmaz, B., Sipahioğrlu, B., Ahmad, N., Unat, D.: Adaptive level binning: a new algorithm for solving sparse triangular systems. In: Proceedings of the International Conference on High Performance Computing in Asia-Pacific Region, pp. 188–198, HPCAsia 2020. Association for Computing Machinery, New York, NY, USA (2020)

Techniques for Managing Polyhedral Dataflow Graphs

Ravi Shankar[1(✉)], Aaron Orenstein[2], Anna Rift[3], Tobi Popoola[3],
MacDonald Lowe[3], Shuai Yang[3], T. Dylan Mikesell[3,4],
and Catherine Olschanowsky[3]

[1] Intel Corporation, Santa Clara, CA, USA
ravi.shankar@intel.com
[2] Case Western University, Cleveland, OH, USA
aao62@case.edu
[3] Boise State University, Boise, ID, USA
{annarift,tobipopoola,macdonaldlowe,shuaiyang}@u.boisestate.edu,
catherineolschan@boisestate.edu
[4] Norwegian Geotechnical Institute, Oslo, Norway
dylan.mikesell@ngi.no

Abstract. Scientific applications, especially legacy applications, contain a wealth of scientific knowledge. As hardware changes, applications need to be ported to new architectures and extended to include scientific advances. As a result, it is common to encounter problems like performance bottlenecks and dead code. A visual representation of the dataflow can help performance experts identify and debug such problems. The Computation API of the sparse polyhedral framework (SPF) provides a single entry point for tools to generate and manipulate polyhedral dataflow graphs, and transform applications. However, when viewing graphs generated for scientific applications there are several barriers. The graphs are large, and manipulating their layout to respect execution order is difficult. This paper presents a case study that uses the Computation API to represent a scientific application, GeoAc, in the SPF. Generated polyhedral dataflow graphs were explored for optimization opportunities and limitations were addressed using several graph simplifications to improve their usability.

Keywords: Sparse Polyhedral Framework · Computation API ·
Polyhedral dataflow graph

1 Introduction

Scientific applications, especially legacy applications, contain a wealth of scientific knowledge. However, older codes need to be ported to new architectures and new generations of computational scientists need to extend them to keep making scientific progress. As applications age and are passed from programmer to programmer, problems creep in: logic and memory bugs, performance bottlenecks, and dead code are just a few of the possibilities. A visual representation

X. Li and S. Chandrasekaran (Eds.): LCPC 2021, LNCS 13181, pp. 134–150, 2022.
https://doi.org/10.1007/978-3-030-99372-6_9

of the code will speed up the learning process for new programmers and can help identify existing issues with the code. Additionally, the right abstraction will allow performance optimizations to be performed by manipulating the visual representation rather than rewriting code manually.

Polyhedral dataflow graphs (PDFGs) [9] highlight the dataflow, data access patterns, and execution schedule for applications visually. Originally developed to identify temporary storage reduction opportunities [15], they have proven to be useful for learning code bases and identifying opportunities for parallelism. Previous efforts used manual drawings of the graphs and then automated graph generation, running only on very small examples. Applying these techniques to real scientific applications remains a significant challenge. This paper uses a scientific application, GeoAc, to explore the limitations of PDFGs and proposes several techniques to ensure correctness and improve their usability.

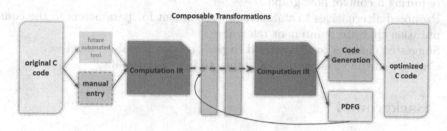

Fig. 1. Optimization pipeline overview [16].

Polyhedral dataflow graphs are part of the Sparse Polyhedral Framework (SPF) and are generated automatically from the SPF intermediate representation [16]. They are referred to as polyhedral because statements are represented as a combination of statements and iteration spaces that are expressed using the polyhedral model. The polyhedral model is a mathematical representation of the source code. Transformations to the execution schedule can be applied using relations. The relations are applied to the iteration spaces, expressed as sets. The resulting code may have a different execution order or different control flow. Importantly, the transformations can be composed. This means that an arbitrarily long series of transformations can be applied to the same code base.

Figure 1 shows the anticipated workflow for human-in-the-loop optimization using PDFGs. Once an application is converted to the SPF intermediate representation, a performance expert examines the resulting graphs, indicates a series of transformations as graph operations, and repeats the process until they are satisfied. Code generation then produces the newly optimized code. It is also possible to automate the choice of transformations. However, automation is not part of the current work.

Previous work demonstrated the concept of PDFGs using manually constructed graphs that represented the execution scheduling using the layout position of nodes and dataflow using edges between nodes. Notably, both data spaces and statements are represented as nodes in the graph. Due to the limitations of this format, the execution schedule does not guide the layout of the graphs as it did in the manually produced graphs. The result is a very large graph. The full PDFG for GeoAc is not readable as it contains 4616 statement nodes and several thousand more data space nodes. The goal of PDFGs is to reveal dataflow optimizations and parallelism opportunities; to make this happen the graphs need to be manipulated to be smaller and communicate key information clearly.

This paper documents the steps taken to process the graphs into more informative and manageable representations. While working with the graphs, we also identified operations needed for correctness. The contributions of this work include:

- A method to transform sections of code to static single assignment without requiring a control flow graph.
- Proposed alternatives to static single assignment for parameters to the computation that are pointers or references.
- Suggested changes to arrays used to pack related variables together.
- Changes to the visualization of graphs to increase usability.

2   Background

This case study uses a portion of a scientific application to explore the capabilities of the Sparse Polyhedral Model and supporting tools. This section describes the application, GeoAc, and reviews important components of the Sparse Polyhedral Model.

2.1   GeoAc

Many earthquakes cause sudden mass displacements at the earth's surface. When this type of earthquake occurs under the ocean, is of strong enough magnitude, and meets certain other criteria, a tsunami is generated. Ground or sea-surface displacements push on the atmosphere, that in turn generates an atmospheric disturbance. This disturbance propagates upward as an acoustic wave eventually inducing a local change in the electron density of the ionosphere. Global Navigation Satellite Systems (GNSS) monitor ionospheric disturbances induced by such phenomena. Such satellite-based remote sensing methods are used to estimate the earth's surface deformation and predict the arrival time of a tsunami.

IonoSeis [12] is a software package that combines multiple existing codebases into a single package to model GNSS-derived electron perturbations in the ionosphere due to the interaction of the neutral atmosphere and charged particles in the ionosphere. One of the pieces of IonoSeis is a ray-tracing package called WASP3D, this is an older tool that does not meet the needs of the workflow. GeoAc [4] is a ray-tracing package developed at Los Alamos National Laboratory that better models the physics, and is the proposed replacement for WASP3D.

The software is written in C++ and models the propagation of acoustic waves through the atmosphere using a fourth-order Runge-Kutta method (RK4). A performance analysis indicates that the RK4 function is the most expensive operation in GeoAc and is thus chosen for further analysis. In this case study, we consider the practical implications of viewing the full RK4 function as a Polyhedral Dataflow Graph. It is to be noted that a newer tool called infraGA/GeoAc that includes an MPI implementation has replaced GeoAc. This work is based on the original code base.

2.2   SPF and the Computation API

The Sparse Polyhedral Framework extends the polyhedral model by supporting non-affine iteration spaces and transforming irregular computations using *uninterpreted functions* [11]. Uninterpreted functions are *symbolic constants* that represent data structures such as the index arrays in sparse data formats. Symbolic constants are constant values that do not change during the course of a computation. The SPF can represent computations with indirect memory accesses, relations with affine constraints, and constraints involving uninterpreted function symbols. The SPF represents *run-time reordering transformations* using integer tuple sets [22,23]. Run-time data reordering techniques attempt to improve the spatial and temporal data locality in a loop by reordering the data based upon the order that it was referenced in the loop [21].

The Computation API [16] is an object-oriented API that provides a precise specification of how to combine the individual components of the SPF to create an intermediate representation. This intermediate representation can produce PDFGs [9] and translates graph operations defined for PDFGs into relations used by the Inspector/Executor Generator Library (IEGenLib) [22]. It can also be passed to Omega [17] for code generation.

IEGenLib is a C++ library with data structures and routines that represent, parse, and visit integer tuple sets and relations with affine constraints and uninterpreted function symbol equality constraints [22]. The Computation API is implemented as a C++ class in IEGenLib and contains all of the components required to express a Computation or a series of Computations. Dense and sparse matrix vector multiplication, shown in Figs. 2 and 4, are used as examples to represent the computations in the SPF.

2.3   Polyhedral Dataflow Graphs

Polyhedral Dataflow graphs [9] represent both the dataflow and execution schedule of a computation. Initially, the graphs were manually drawn using the polyhedral representation as a guide. The current version of the graph is automatically generated. The SPF Computation intermediate representation is visited and a dot format graph is created.

Figures 3, 5 show the corresponding PDFGs that are generated using the intermediate representation created in Figs. 2 and 4. Multiple node types connected by edges comprise the graphs. These node type are variations of statement

Dense Matrix vector multiply

```
1  /* Dense vector multiply
2  for (i = 0; i < N; i++) {
3      for (j=0; j<M; j++) {
4          y[i] += A[i][j] * x[j];
5  }}*/
6  Computation* denseComp = new Computation();
7  denseComp->addDataSpace("y", "int*");
8  denseComp->addDataSpace("A", "int*");
9  denseComp->addDataSpace("x", "int*");
10 Stmt* denseS0 = new Stmt(
11     "y(i) += A(i,j) * x(j);", // Source code
12     "{[i,j]: 0 <= i < N && 0 <= j < M}", // Iteration domain
13     "{[i,j] ->[0,i,0,j,0]}", // Scheduling Function
14     { {"y", "{[i,j]->[i]}"}, {"A", "{[i,j]->[i,j]}"},
15       {"x", "{[i,j]->[j]}"} }, // Data reads
16     { {"y", "{[i,j]->[i]}"} } ); // Data writes
17 denseComp->addStmt(denseS0);
```

Fig. 2. Dense matrix vector multiply represented using the computation API.

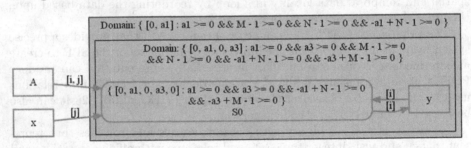

Fig. 3. PDFG for dense matrix vector multiply. A, x, y are data spaces, S0 is a statement, and the Domain: labels indicate loop levels.

or data space nodes. Node types include: statements, data spaces, read-only parameters, parameters, active-out data spaces, read-only-active-out parameters, and active-out parameters.

A statement node is represented as a rectangle with rounded edges. It has an execution schedule, a statement number, and potentially a debug string. We generate the execution schedule by applying the scheduling function to the iteration space. For example, the statement node in Fig. 5 executes the statement referred to using macro $S0$ with the execution schedule $\{[0, a1, 0, a3, 0] : a1 \geq 0 \wedge a3 \geq 0 \wedge -a1 + N - 1 \geq 0 \wedge -a3 + M - 1 \geq 0\}$. This is generated by applying the scheduling function $\{[i, k, j]- > [0, i, 0, k, 0, j, 0]\}$ to the iteration space $\{[i, k, j] : 0 \leq i < N \wedge rowptr(i) \leq k < rowptr(i + 1) \wedge j = col(k)\}$. Code generation uses execution schedules to lexicographically order the statements.

```
   Sparse matrix vector multiply

 1 /*Sparse vector multiply
 2 for (i = 0; i < N; i++) {
 3    for (k=rowptr[i]; k<rowptr[i+1]; k++) {
 4        j = col[k];
 5        y[i] += A[k] * x[j];
 6 }}*/
 7 Computation* sparseComp = new Computation();
 8 sparseComp->addDataSpace("y", "int*");
 9 sparseComp->addDataSpace("A", "int*");
10 sparseComp->addDataSpace("x", "int*");
11 Stmt* sparseS0 = new Stmt(
12   "y(i) += A(k) * x(j)", // Source code
13   // iteration domain
14   "{[i,k,j]: 0<=i<N && rowptr(i)<=k<rowptr(i+1) && j=col(k)}",
15   "{[i,k,j]->[0,i,0,k,0,j,0]}", // Scheduling Function
16   { {"y", "{[i,k,j]->[i]}"},{"A", "{[i,k,j]->[k]}"},
17     {"x", "{[i,k,j]->[j]}"}}, // Data reads
18   { {"y", "{[i,k,j]->[i]}"} } // Data writes
19 );
20 sparseComp->addStmt(sparseS0);
```

Fig. 4. Sparse matrix vector multiply represented using the Computation API.

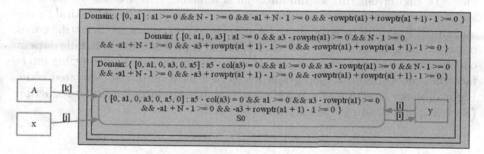

Fig. 5. PDFG for sparse matrix vector multiply. A, x, y are data spaces, S0 is a statement, and the Domain: labels indicate loop levels.

All edges represent reads and writes to data spaces by statement nodes. The labels on edges refer to the access parameters. All scalar values are read and written using 0 as an access parameter. Arrays can be read and written using any combination of constants or iterators from the iteration space.

Data space nodes are drawn as rectangles with sharp corners. The representation splits data space nodes into the types listed above. In static single assignment form, every data space should have only one edge pointing into it. An exception is made for parameters to the computation that are pointers or references. Shaded rectangles surround groups of statements that are executed in a common loop nest. A partial form of polyhedral scanning is used to establish the encapsulating spaces. Visually, this helps identify sections of the code that are executed more than once, and are more important for performance.

3   Case Study: Expressing GeoAc and Examining Polyhedral Dataflow Graphs

This case study mimics the behavior of a future automated tool (shown in Fig. 1) that will consume existing C code and produce the SPF intermediate representation. In this work, calls to the Computation API are manually written to create the intermediate representation. The SPF tool chain generates code from the intermediate representation and generates the graphs presented in the case study. Results from executing the generated code were compared with those of the original to ensure correctness.

The case study drove the development of the Computation API and demonstrated several shortcomings of PDFGs for a full scientific application. This section overviews the challenges overcome to create accurate dataflow graphs using a sparse polyhedral representation. The first challenge was to create an approximation to static single assignment in the absence of a control flow graph. Special handling of structs, pass-by-reference or pointer parameters, and some arrays was required. The size of the graphs make them almost impossible to view. To circumvent this we minimize all statements that are not within loops and propose future analysis to further simplify the graphs. The polyhedral model and the SPF require constraints to be affine based on constants. Scientific codes often use data in control flow. We expanded our representation to handle data in constraints in limited circumstances. Finally, we implemented a debugging interface that can be used to map graph nodes to a location in the generated code. Figure 6 shows a section of a graph after applying producer-consumer reduction (Sect. 3.2) and dead code elimination (Sect. 3.5).

Fig. 6. A subsection of the graph with producer-consumer reductions and dead code elimination applied. The pink node is a parameter that is written to within the loop level. (Color figure online)

3.1 Approximate Static Single Assignment

The Computation API and polyhedral dataflow graphs support intrinsic types, pointers, and references. User defined types (structs and classes) are not supported. Scientific codes commonly make extensive use of user defined types. All structs and classes must be flattened. All GeoAc structs were converted to a set of data spaces: one corresponding to each member variable. This alteration was done before using the computation API. The consequence is that any tool generating calls to the API is responsible for object flattening. These restrictions allow memory allocation to be delayed until after code generation. The memory allocation is preprended to the source code. Macros map between the actual memory and the data space names used in the representation.

The computation is converted to SSA form as it is built. As each statement is added, the reads and writes are inspected and stored. If the data space written to by a statement was written to by a previous statement, the data space of the previous statement gets a revision number. Affected reads are updated as well. Importantly, the intermediate representation does not keep a control flow graph and ϕ or join nodes must be added to ensure proper versioning.

To generate ϕ nodes in the absence of a control flow graph we use the constraints on iteration spaces. We use a dominance frontier method [8] adapted for use with the polyhedral model rather than a control flow graph. If foo is a data space that requires a ϕ node as in Fig. 7, we must locate three statements:

1. **read statement** - The statement that reads from foo
2. **first write** - The most recent write to foo under any constraints
3. **guaranteed write** - The most recent write to foo whose constraints also apply to the read statement.

ϕ Node Example

```
1 foo = 0; // SSA: foo_0 = 0; (guaranteed write)
2 if (i - 1 >= N) {
3     foo = 1; // SSA: foo_1 = 1; (first write)
4 }
5 // SSA: add phi node foo = -N + i - 1 >= 0 ? foo_1 : foo_0;
6 bar = foo; // read statement
```

Fig. 7. ϕ node example.

We begin with the read statement and move backwards through our statements, identifying the first and guaranteed writes. We construct a ϕ node if the first and guaranteed writes are distinct statements. We extract all conditions that apply to the first write but not to the read statement. The ϕ node takes the general form: `foo = conditions ? first write : guaranteed write;`.

Due to SSA, the guaranteed write is versioned while first write is left alone. The
addition of the ϕ node provides a new write to foo and versions the first write.
This means all three statements write to different versions of foo. Figure 8 shows
the dataflow graph generated from the ϕ node example in Fig. 7.

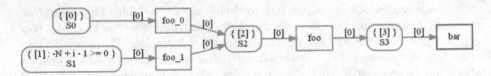

Fig. 8. Graph generated from Fig. 7. `foo` is written to once as `foo_0` (S0) and once as
`foo_1`(S1). `foo` then chooses between these values based on the given condition (S2)
and is subsequently read by `bar` (S3).

Parameters that are pointer or reference types have to be handled differ-
ently. Any parameters of those types can be rewritten multiple times. As part of
SSA, the final write to a data space remains unversioned—only previous writes
are versioned. Thus at the end of their dataflow, these parameters retain their
original names and are then correctly recognized as active-out data spaces. It
is important to consider the execution schedule when examining these nodes in
the dataflow graphs as this could allow for illegal schedule transformations to be
applied.

3.2 Producer Consumer Reductions

A producer-consumer relationship that can be safely excluded from the visual
representation of the graph exists between some statements $S0$ and $S1$ through
a data space $D0$ if:

- $S0$ only writes to $D0$
- $D0$ is only written to by $S0$
- $D0$ is only read by $S1$

An example is shown in Fig. 9a.

Hiding these simple chains of statements in the graph is similar to group-
ing statements into basic blocks. This operation should not be mistaken for a
producer-consumer fusion. The reduction improves graph readability but does
not change the actual computation. The steps of the reduction process are:

- $S0$'s reads are assigned to $S1$.
- $D0$ is removed as a read from $S1$.
- $S0$ and $D0$ are removed from the graph.

An example result is shown in Fig. 9b.

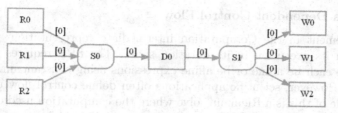

(a) A dataflow graph with a producer-consumer relationship between $S0$ and $S1$.

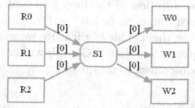

(b) The dataflow graph after producer-consumer fusion.

Fig. 9. Producer-consumer fusion example. R's: reads and W's: writes.

3.3 Graph Components

Within a dataflow graph, there are multiple types of nodes that require distinction. Statements and data spaces are the primary types, denoted by curved and sharp-cornered rectangles, respectively. Statements do not require further classification as they only serve to connect data spaces with a line of code. Data spaces have multiple types: normal, parameter, and active-out. Normal is equivalent to neither parameter nor active-out. From the latter two, we derive active-out parameter, read-only parameter, and read-only active-out parameter. Note that pass-by-reference parameters are active-out parameters and returned values are active-out non-parameters. If a data space is never read from and not active-out, we call it an unread data space. Such data spaces are the target of dead code elimination. Finally, we organize statements into loop levels, corresponding to loops in the source code. Each data space is placed in the loop level of the statement that write to it. We encapsulate grouped nodes in a filled-in gray box with black edges. See Fig. 10 for the graph components.

Fig. 10. The different types of components and their colorings

3.4   Data Dependent Control Flow

Each statement in the Computation intermediate representation stores constraints on its execution in its iteration space. The SPF requires that those constraints each be affine or be affine expressions using constant uninterpreted functions. However, scientific applications often define control flow using data. An example of this is a Riemann solve where the computation used depends on the value at that iteration [3]. We support constraints on data by requiring that they are constant for the duration of the loop nest and treating them as uninterpreted functions. Transformations can be performed in the presence of these constraints, but cannot use them. This is a feature we will explore in the future. One limitation of this approach is that IEGenLib will not support $\neq$ constraints as this would create a non-convex iteration space.

3.5   Dead Code Elimination

Eliminating redundant computations is an optimization technique that improves the performance of an application. In a graph, a statement node is dead if it writes to a data node that is never read from. In our work, we provide this transformation as an option to the Computation intermediate representation. It should be noted that this operation removes dead statements from the Computation intermediate representation. We implement this functionality by performing a breadth first search from dead data nodes in the graph, we keep removing statement nodes recursively until we reach data nodes that are read from by other statements. A breadth first approach allows our algorithm to remove dead statements per each level when traversing the graph backwards. This operation results in a significantly smaller dataflow graph.

3.6   Subgraphs

Due to the immense size of the dataflow graph it is very difficult to visually inspect the dependencies of a single node. To aid in this, it is helpful to remove edges and nodes not connected to the target node. More formally, we define a dependency relationship between node A and node B if B can reach A through either only in-edges or only out-edges. B may reach A through a combination of in and out-edges, however this only implies that B and A share read/write dependencies, not that one depends on the output of the other. We say A has a write dependency with B if B can reach A using only in-edges. We say A has a read dependency with B if B can reach A using only out-edges. Practically, a read dependency indicates that A uses B's output and a write dependency indicates B uses A's output. Figure 11 shows the read dependencies for data space _iegen39_iegen_31X.

3.7   Constant Size Arrays

One coding pattern observed in scientific applications such as GeoAc is packing individual, but related scalar variables into constant sized arrays. The code then

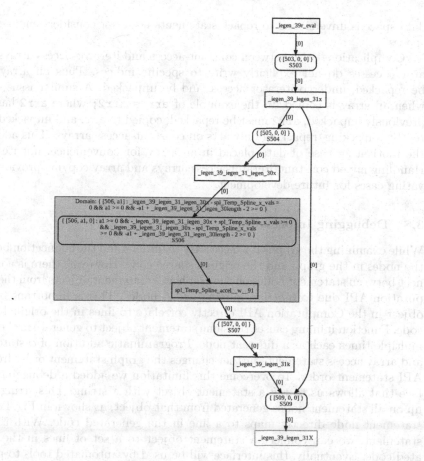

Fig. 11. The read dependencies for _iegen39_iegen_31X (highlighted in yellow). (Color figure online)

accesses the variables using constants or iterators, the latter often occurring in loops with small domains.

In our SSA form, arrays are versioned as a whole, meaning that writing to a single index versions the entire array. This causes extra versioning that complicates the view of the dataflow and generates incorrect code. One solution is to detect arrays that are only accessed using literals and replace them with individual variables. Array accesses using variables whose values can be determined at compile time are also replaced. This process replaces each array access with a data space, combining the array name and indices as follows: $arr[i_0][i_1]...[i_n] \rightarrow arr\_ati_1\_ati_2....ati_n$. If reading from the array, unpacking adds a statement of the form arr_at0_at1 = arr[0][1];". SSA safely renames the new data spaces. At the end of the computation, repacking generates statements of the form arr[0][1] = arr_at0_at1;. With SSA, the last write to a data space is unversioned so repack statements need not consider renamed data spaces.

Complications arise between constant-access and iterator-access arrays. Iterator accesses do not explicitly write to specific indices. Thus an array must be repacked, undergo iterator access, and be unpacked. A similar issue occurs when an array is copied. In the example of `arr = arr2;` where `arr2` has been previously unpacked, `arr2` must be repacked, copied to `arr`, and unpacked. Currently, unpacking/repacking only acts on constant-access arrays. This addresses the motivating case of data placed in an array for convenience, not iteration. Handling mixed constant/iterator-access arrays and array copying provide motivating cases for future development.

3.8 Debugging Information

While examining the graphs it is necessary to understand the connection between the nodes in the graph and the original source code. However, there is a disconnect between statement nodes on the graph and statement objects from the Computation API due to function inlining and ϕ nodes. This is important because object in the Computation API directly correlate to lines in the original source code. Function inlining causes the same statement object to generate in the graph multiple times each as a different node. Programmatic addition of ϕ statements and array access statements further changes the graph statement order from the API statement order. To overcome this limitation we added a debugging interface that allows us to tag a statement object with a string. This string shows up on all statement nodes generated from that object, as shown in Fig. 12. Each statement node directly maps to a line in the generated code. With a debug statement, we can connect a statement object to a set of lines in the generated code. Eventually, this interface will be used by automated tools to provide filename and line number information from the original input code.

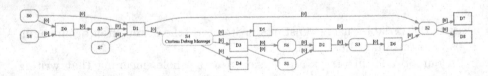

Fig. 12. An example graph that includes a debug statement at $S4$ (highlighted green for easy identification). In the scalable vector graphic format, the user-defined debug string is searchable for easy node identification. (Color figure online)

4 Related Work

This work builds on previous work that can be divided into 3 categories: polyhedral tools, sparse polyhedral tools, and similar macro dataflow graphs. Because this work is based on the sparse polyhedral model, the graphs are capable of representing both regular and irregular computations. Additionally, using a scientific application in a use case reveals many of the issues related to graph size. The graphs and associated tool chain build on previous work building the Computation API [16], designing polyhedral dataflow graphs [9], and underlying tools CHiLL [7], IEGenLib [23], and Omega [17].

Polyhedral Tools such as PolyMage [14], Halide [13,18,19] and AlphaZ [24] use the polyhedral model to transform regular codes. PolyMage and Halide are domain specific languages and compilers for optimizing parallelism, locality, and recomputation in image processing pipelines. Halide separates the definition of algorithms from the concerns of optimization making them simpler, more modular and more portable. PolyMage's optimization strategy relies primarily on the transformation and code generation capabilities of the polyhedral compiler framework and performs complex fusion, tiling, and storage optimization automatically. AlphaZ [24] expresses transformations using the Alpha equational language and allows for complex memory remapping. Our work differs from the aforementioned work due to our support for non affine polyhedral spaces characteristic with sparse computations.

Work done on representing indirect memory accesses in a computation using the polyhedral model has seen the development of tools such as Omega [10], Chill [7] and the Computation API [16]. Omega [10] is a C++ library for manipulating integer tuple relations and sets. Codegen+ [6] is built on omega and generates code with polyhedral scanning in the presence of uninterpreted functions. Chill [7] is a polyhedral compiler transformation and code generation framework that uses Codegen+ for code generation. It allows users to specify transformation sequences through scripts. Our work differs from this work as we represent a holistic view of a computation and we support more precise transformations in the presence of sparse computations.

Existing work demonstrates the benefit of polyhedral dataflow optimizations. Olschanowsky et al. demonstrated this benefit on a computational fluid dynamic benchmark [15]. Davis et al. automated the experiments from the previous work using modified macro dataflow graphs [9]. This work distinguishes itself by being applied to a full application in a different domain. The Concurrent Collections (CnC) programming model [5] is a dataflow and stream-processing language where a program is a graph of computation nodes that communicate with each other. DFGR [20] is based on CnC and Habanero-C [1] programming models and allows developers to express programs at a high level with dataflow graphs as an intermediate representation. Our work uses the dataflow graph to focus on serial code optimization while DFGR and CnC explores parallelism. Stateful dataflow multigraphs (SDFGs) [2] are a data-centric intermediate representation that enables separating code definition from its optimization. Our work differ from SDFGs due to the use of the polyhedral model. The graphs are not the intermediate representation, but a view of that representation. Any graph operation performed to transform the graph is translated to relations and applied to the underlying polyhedral representation.

5   Conclusion

This paper presents a case study that uses the Computation API to represent a scientific application, GeoAc, in the sparse polyhedral framework. Polyhedral dataflow graphs were generated from the Computation intermediate representation and measures were taken to make the graphs more readable and informative. The computation is converted to SSA form as it is built to simplify and enable optimizations like redundancy elimination. In the absence of control flow, constraints on the iteration space were used to generate ϕ nodes for data space versioning. The large size of the generated graph is made more manageable by minimizing non-loop statements to keep the graphs simple and easy to read. Function inlining by the Computation API makes it difficult to map the source code to the generated code. This limitation is overcome by adding a debugging interface that can tag statement objects created from the source code with a string that is then searchable in the graph. PDFGs are generated using the dot format, making the layout of the graph dependent on the dataflow rather than execution order. The graph is displayed left to right and different colors are used to distinguish various graphical elements.

Acknowledgements. This material is based upon work supported by the National Science Foundation under Grant Numbers 1849463 and 1563818. This research utilized the high-performance computing support of the R2 compute cluster (DOI: 10.18122/B2S41H) provided by Boise State University's Research Computing Department.

References

1. Barik, R., et al.: The habanero multicore software research project. In: Proceedings of the 24th ACM SIGPLAN Conference Companion on Object Oriented Programming Systems Languages and Applications, OOPSLA 2009, pp. 735–736. Association for Computing Machinery, New York (2009). https://doi.org/10.1145/1639950.1639989
2. Ben-Nun, T., de Fine Licht, J., Ziogas, A.N., Schneider, T., Hoefler, T.: Stateful dataflow multigraphs: a data-centric model for performance portability on heterogeneous architectures. In: Proceedings of the International Conference for High Performance Computing, Networking, Storage and Analysis, SC 2019. Association for Computing Machinery, New York (2019). https://doi.org/10.1145/3295500.3356173
3. Benabderrahmane, M.-W., Pouchet, L.-N., Cohen, A., Bastoul, C.: The polyhedral model is more widely applicable than you think. In: Gupta, R. (ed.) CC 2010. LNCS, vol. 6011, pp. 283–303. Springer, Heidelberg (2010). https://doi.org/10.1007/978-3-642-11970-5_16
4. Blom, P.: GeoAc: numerical tools to model acoustic propagation in the geometric limit (2014). https://github.com/LANL-Seismoacoustics/GeoAc
5. Budimlić, Z., et al.: Concurrent collections. Sci. Program. **18**(3–4), 203–217 (2010)

6. Chen, C.: Polyhedra scanning revisited. In: Proceedings of the 33rd ACM SIG-PLAN Conference on Programming Language Design and Implementation, PLDI 2012, pp. 499–508. Association for Computing Machinery, New York (2012). https://doi.org/10.1145/2254064.2254123

7. Chen, C., Chame, J., Hall, M.: CHiLL: a framework for composing high-level loop transformations. Technical report (2008)

8. Cytron, R., Ferrante, J., Rosen, B.K., Wegman, M.N., Zadeck, F.K.: An efficient method of computing static single assignment form. In: Proceedings of the 16th ACM SIGPLAN-SIGACT Symposium on Principles of Programming Languages, POPL 1989, pp. 25–35. Association for Computing Machinery, New York (1989). https://doi.org/10.1145/75277.75280

9. Davis, E.C., Strout, M.M., Olschanowsky, C.: Transforming loop chains via macro dataflow graphs. In: Proceedings of the 2018 International Symposium on Code Generation and Optimization, pp. 265–277. ACM (2018)

10. Kelly, W., Maslov, V., Pugh, W., Rosser, E., Shpeisman, T., Wonnacott, D.: The Omega Library interface guide (1995)

11. LaMielle, A., Strout, M.M.: Enabling code generation within the sparse polyhedral framework. Technical report, Technical Report CS-10-102 (2010)

12. Mikesell, T., Rolland, L., Lee, R., Zedek, F., Coïsson, P., Dessa, J.X.: IonoSeis: a package to model coseismic ionospheric disturbances. Atmosphere 10(8), 443 (2019)

13. Mullapudi, R.T., Adams, A., Sharlet, D., Ragan-Kelley, J., Fatahalian, K.: Automatically scheduling Halide image processing pipelines. ACM Trans. Graph. (TOG) 35(4), 83 (2016)

14. Mullapudi, R.T., Vasista, V., Bondhugula, U.: PolyMage: automatic optimization for image processing pipelines. ACM SIGARCH Comput. Archit. News 43, 429–443 (2015)

15. Olschanowsky, C., Strout, M.M., Guzik, S., Loffeld, J., Hittinger, J.: A study on balancing parallelism, data locality, and recomputation in existing PDE solvers. In: Proceedings of the International Conference for High Performance Computing, Networking, Storage and Analysis, pp. 793–804. IEEE Press, New York (2014)

16. Popoola, T., et al.: An object-oriented interface to the sparse polyhedral library. In: 2021 IEEE 45th Annual Computers, Software, and Applications Conference (COMPSAC), pp. 1825–1831 (2021). https://doi.org/10.1109/COMPSAC51774.2021.00275

17. Pugh, W., Wonnacott, D.: Eliminating false data dependences using the omega test. In: Proceedings of the ACM SIGPLAN 1992 Conference on Programming Language Design and Implementation, PLDI 1992, pp. 140–151. Association for Computing Machinery, New York (1992). https://doi.org/10.1145/143095.143129

18. Ragan-Kelley, J., Adams, A., Paris, S., Levoy, M., Amarasinghe, S., Durand, F.: Decoupling algorithms from schedules for easy optimization of image processing pipelines (2012)

19. Ragan-Kelley, J., Barnes, C., Adams, A., Paris, S., Durand, F., Amarasinghe, S.: Halide: a language and compiler for optimizing parallelism, locality, and recomputation in image processing pipelines. ACM SIGPLAN Not. 48(6), 519–530 (2013)

20. Sbirlea, A., Pouchet, L.N., Sarkar, V.: DFGR an intermediate graph representation for macro-dataflow programs. In: 2014 4th Workshop on Data-Flow Execution Models for Extreme Scale Computing, pp. 38–45 (2014). https://doi.org/10.1109/DFM.2014.9

21. Strout, M.M., Carter, L., Ferrante, J.: Compile-time composition of run-time data and iteration reorderings. SIGPLAN Not. **38**(5), 91–102 (2003). https://doi.org/10.1145/780822.781142
22. Strout, M.M., Georg, G., Olschanowsky, C.: Set and relation manipulation for the sparse polyhedral framework. In: Kasahara, H., Kimura, K. (eds.) LCPC 2012. LNCS, vol. 7760, pp. 61–75. Springer, Heidelberg (2013). https://doi.org/10.1007/978-3-642-37658-0_5
23. Strout, M.M., LaMielle, A., Carter, L., Ferrante, J., Kreaseck, B., Olschanowsky, C.: An approach for code generation in the sparse polyhedral framework. Parallel Comput. **53**, 32–57 (2016)
24. Yuki, T., Gupta, G., Kim, D.G., Pathan, T., Rajopadhye, S.: AlphaZ: a system for design space exploration in the polyhedral model. In: Kasahara, H., Kimura, K. (eds.) LCPC 2012. LNCS, vol. 7760, pp. 17–31. Springer, Heidelberg (2013). https://doi.org/10.1007/978-3-642-37658-0_2

Author Index

Printed in the United States
by Baker & Taylor Publisher Services